THE
AGV HANDBOOK

THE
AGV HANDBOOK

Roberto F. Lu.
Summer 1, 1993

A HANDBOOK FOR THE SELECTION OF
AUTOMATED GUIDED VEHICLE SYSTEMS

BY
GUY A. CASTLEBERRY, PE

Braun-Brumfield, Inc.
Ann Arbor, Michigan

Distributed by: AGV Decisions, Incorporated
3613 East Norport Drive
Port Washington, Wisconsin   53074

Braun-Brumfield, Inc.
Ann Arbor, Michigan

To all the people who have helped me throughout my career and life, but especially to Sarah, who has taught me the value of persistence, and to Ben, who has taught me the value of asking questions.

Guy Castleberry
Isaiah 40:8

CONTRIBUTING COMPANIES

The following companies contributed all of the photographs and most of the illustrations used throughout the book.

Apogee Robotics
2643 Midpoint Drive
Fort Collins, Colorado 80525

Caterpillar Industrial Inc.
5960 Heisley Road
Mentor, Ohio 44060

Clark Material Handling Company
333 West Vine Street
Lexington, Kentucky 40507

Control Engineering Company
Harbor Springs Road
Harbor Springs, Michigan 49740

Eaton-Kenway
515 East 100 South Street
Salt Lake City, Utah 84102

Eisenmann Corporation
Material Handling Systems
150 East Dartmoor Drive
Crystal Lake, Illinois 60014

Elwell-Parker Electric Company
4205 St. Clair Avenue
Cleveland, Ohio 44103

FATA Automation (USA)
37050 Industrial Road
Livonia, Michigan 48150

FMC Corporation
Material Handling Systems Division
400 Highpoint Drive
Chalfont, Pennsylvania 18914

Hyster Company
P.O. Box 2902
Portland, Oregon 97208

Litton Industrial Automation
Material Handling Division
2300 Litton Lane
Hebron, Kentucky 41048

Mannesmann Demag
Material Handling System Division
2660 28th Street S.E.
Grand Rapids, Michigan 49508

Mentor AGVS, Incorporated
8500 Station Street
Mentor, Ohio 44060

Murata of America
1250 Rankin Street
Suite D
Troy, Michigan 48083

The Raymond Corporation
Corporate Headquarters
Greene, New York 13778

Roberts Corporation
A Cross & Trecker Company
P.O. Box 40760
3001 West Main Street
Lansing, Michigan 48901

TransLogic Corporation
10825 East 47th Avenue
Denver, Colorado 80239-2913

Resources, to produce results, must be allocated to opportunities rather than problems.

Peter Drucker

CONTENTS

INTRODUCTION

The purpose of *The AGV Handbook* is to present a practical, "how-to" guide for selecting an automated guided vehicle (AGV) material handling system. The book addresses automated guided vehicles and their role in material handling and factory automation. Thus, a major portion of this book is a collection and presentation of rules, guidelines, techniques, procedures, and formulas; this information will guide an effective evaluation of the state-of-the-art of AGV systems.

AGVs have engendered a prodigious amount of interest in industry throughout the world. The primary reason for this interest is the benefits of AGV technology: cost reduction, improved operating efficiency, less inventory investment, flexibility to accommodate future changes, and increased reliability of the material handling system.

As AGV products have proliferated, the ability to select the correct vehicle type and system technology for the application has become more complicated. To simplify the selection process, *The AGV Handbook* has been written to provide a basic understanding of the technology, telling how these systems work and how to get the most out of them.

Most materials written on AGVs describe only a small aspect of the total subject. The information presented in *The AGV Handbook* is comprehensive, discussing in detail the vital issues that must be considered in selecting an AGV system. This book should help companies—engineers, purchasing agents, and operation personnel—make better AGV decisions.

In *The AGV Handbook* the reader will learn about the concepts and technology of AGVs. The specific information will:

- Discuss the application of AGVs in assembly systems, flexible manufacturing systems, distribution systems, and in general industry.

- Identify the benefits and justification of using AGVs.

- Discuss the three categories of AGV systems as they relate to call requests, dispatching of vehicles, and level of controls.

- Discuss the major vehicle types, important vehicle attributes, typical applications, and general vehicle descriptions.

- Devote a complete chapter to the components that make up a vehicle, including types of guidance systems, measuring wheels, common steering wheel geometries, antennas, and much more.

- Explore the types of battery charging methods used to restore the vehicles' power.

- Present the AGV system control philosophy and hierarchy for centralized and decentralized control systems.

- Discuss in detail the different communication methods, including radio communication, infrared light communication, and inductive communication.

- Cover the importance of system safety, identifying the five basic safety mechanisms which must be incorporated into every system to insure a safe working system.

• Discuss the methods to be used in sizing the AGV system for the plant where the system will be used. Formulas will be given, and important definitions will be explained.

• Provide pricing guidelines for determining the budget for different AGV systems.

The ultimate purpose of *The AGV Handbook* is to help the reader make a better decision, selecting the correct AGV material handling system for the user's needs. A good decision is never an accident; it is always the result of careful evaluation, a thorough understanding of the AGV technology, and the correct choice of the many alternatives.

Guy A. Castleberry, P.E.

Figure 1.1 AGV transfers automobile bodies through the plant as they are built. When the AGV moves into the welding station, locaters align the pallet carried by the vehicle. After the alignment is secured, the robots start their weld process. These vehicles have been specially designed to operate in a hostile welding environment. (Courtesy of FATA Automation, Livonia, Michigan)

1 A MANUFACTURING RENAISSANCE

High technology is reinventing the factory and beginning to reshape United States industry. These plants can build a wide variety of high-quality products and switch from one product to another on signal from a central computer; thus the beginning of a manufacturing renaissance.

There is an urgency in this country to automate the manufacturing process; this task has been described as a matter of national survival. Nearly every company that wants to compete in today's world market must plan to implement some type of automation in their factories. The factory is re-emerging as the focal point of corporate strategy—after two decades of neglect in most industries. There are ever-growing pressures to improve productivity, flexibility, delivery times, costs, quality, and customer service.

In most competitive manufacturing and non-manufacturing environments, an effective material handling transportation system is essential. Before the product reaches the consumer or industrial user, it spends most of its time in storage or being transported. This handling and storage cost can be as much as 30% of the manufacturing costs; therefore material handling systems offer a substantial potential to reduce production costs. The main objective for the future must be high production quality at low production costs, combined with the ability to offer better working conditions for employees. Automated guided vehicles can assist most companies in reaching this objective—it is a tool for the pursuit of profits.

In the factory of the future, robots, automated material handling systems, and computer-controlled machines, working together with computerized planning, scheduling, materials transportation, inventory control, and tool management systems, will be able to perform many of the manufacturing operations that now require human skills. This will have an enormous impact on productivity. On the basis of 40 hours per shift, automated factories will be able to operate around the clock, a full 168 hours a week, or the equivalent of four 40-hour shifts a week. This alone would produce a 100% productivity and utilization of equipment gain over that of most factories today, which operate only two shifts per week.

One of the largest areas of growth in industrial automation is materials handling, which is a key element in achieving the full benefit of factory automation. One of the most dynamic technologies contributing to this growth is the automated guided vehicle system (AGVS). An automated guided vehicle (AGV) is an unmanned vehicle capable of following an external guidance signal to deliver a unit load from destination to destination. AGVs are extremely flexible in application and function because 1) there are many types of vehicles, 2) the vehicles are software driven and not hardware driven, and 3) many levels of intelligence are available for controlling a wide range of systems, from the simple to the complex.

AGV History

Automated guided vehicles have been around for more than 30 years. The first AGV system was introduced and built in 1953; it was a modified towing tractor used to pull a trailer and follow an overhead wire in a grocery warehouse.

In 1959, towing AGVs were introduced and operated in factories and warehouses.

In 1973, Volvo in Kalmar, Sweden, developed 280 computer-controlled assembly vehicles for a new factory. The original goal was not to develop a material handling system, but instead to develop non-synchronous assembly equipment as an alternative to the conventional conveyor assembly line.

The introduction of the unit load vehicle in the mid 1970s was the first big development for the automated guided vehicle industry. These unit load AGVs have gained widespread acceptance in the material handling marketplace because they serve several functions: a work platform, a transportation device, and a link in the control and information system for the factory. Today there are several hundred systems in operation using unit load vehicles, produced by a number of manufacturers, transporting materials in warehouses, factories, mills, and other industrial and commercial settings.

The biggest impact on the development of AGVs came from the powerful microprocessor and control technology which became available at acceptable prices in the late 1970s. This technology has been responsible for the advancement of AGV systems, providing more flexibility and capability.

Like all high-technology products based on electronic and computer software, AGVs have been influenced by the market explosion of microcomputers and microelectronics. The computers used in AGV systems can store instructions, make decisions, and execute procedures. In practice, AGV systems are capable of performing almost all of the decisions and control functions currently done by humans in managing the material handling process: schedule factory time, maintain inventories, manage the system details, and control many types of mechanical systems in the overall operation.

The use of AGVs is changing drastically from traditional distribution-oriented applications to complex computer-controlled automobile assembly systems with robotic interfaces. They can be stand-alone systems, or be an integral part of another system and bring islands of automation together. Originally designed for horizontal transportation of palletized material, vehicles and controls are now as varied as industrial robots. Improved methods of load movement are complimented with computer tracking on the shop floor. At the unsophisticated end, an AGV system replaces the labor-intensive fork truck or manual movement of material. Market acceptance has given AGV systems the application variety needed to expand into a standard accepted material handling method in many industries.

The market demand for AGVs can be measured by the number of AGV manufacturers. In the late 1970s there were fewer than six AGV vendors in the United States, and only three types of vehicles. In 1990 there are more than 40 vendors and more than 15 vehicle types, with an increasing emphasis on standard design.

The trend during this and the next decade will be to use AGVs in assembly applications, with smaller systems used in the general cross section of industries. The systems are applied to products which have parts added in a serial assembly process, such as automotive engine or automotive transmission assembly, and truck body assembly. AGV assembly systems are now being extended to many other types of products. In all these applications people are much more involved, playing a larger role. All this change is taking place in the pursuit of increased productivity and manufacturing efficiency.

BENEFITS USING AGVS

Flexibility The primary advantage of an AGV is its adaptability and flexibility, established over the years by the many AGV systems installed without major changes in existing facility layout or material flow. AGV systems add flexibility to the material handling process in a manufacturing environment, providing good management control. This flexibility reduces the risks of obsolescence and increases the utilization of the complete automation system and factory.

It should be noted that while more manufacturers, consultants, and engineers talk about flexibility, it is at the expense of simplicity. The more flexibility required in the system, the more costly and more complex the sub-systems. The general rule of thumb: don't specify more flexibility than is absolutely required, and when in doubt, simplify.

The flexibility of AGV systems is extensive and can be broken down into several areas:

Volume Flexibility A multiple vehicle system provides extraordinary reaction to variations in the production volumes as compared to other material handling systems. With an AGV, product sequencing can be random; any product can be computer-directed to any destination within the system.

Schedule Flexibility The versatility of material handling by AGVs allows any production schedules to be met with a high level of reliability, and any last-minute changes in the schedule can be accommodated in the master schedule. These systems are dynamic.

Recovery Flexibility If a vehicle fails or a peripheral machine or station malfunctions, the system can continue to deliver materials, using alternate routes to each pickup and delivery station. This benefit can also be achieved with fixed-base material handling equipment, but it is expensive, takes a considerable amount of floor space, and is a permanent obstruction.

Hardware Flexibility After a system has been installed, it is easy to increase the number of vehicles, guidepath routes, and pickup and delivery stations. It's easy to change the guidepath layout and install additional buffer storage, compared to other systems, thus providing greater flexibility without path restriction or obstruction. Storage racks or any type of storage device can be put where required without being close to either shipping or receiving.

AGV systems can replace conventional industrial trucks, and be added to facilities where continuous conveyors are too inflexible or unsuitable.

Software Flexibility AGVs can be reprogrammed and retrofitted with new tooling to meet changing needs. Making changes in software to reprogram the vehicles and system functions is easy. Soft automation simply requires new instructions or programs to be put into the vehicle and/or system controller. This greatly reduces the time and cost of altering the material handling system.

Also, the system software can produce the reports and the status of inventories necessary for good management control of the operation.

Vehicle Flexibility Numerous vehicle types are available for a wide range of industrial applications, with the ability to perform a variety of operations. AGVs can store palletized loads in racks, pick up palletized loads from the floor, position palletized loads on load stands, and provide unlimited horizontal transportation of material.

Real-Time Control The real-time control improves the system's ability to respond to manufacturing requests, maintain up-to-date work-in-process, maintain up-to-date inventory, and reduce overall inventory requirements of the plant.

Floor Space Savings AGVs make efficient use of floor space. Although the saving in floor space is difficult to identify in the justification phase of the AGV project, this saving leads to more efficient material flow, a reduction of work-in-process, and less production area floor space used to store materials.

AGV systems need less floor space than conventional conveyor systems because they eliminate large fix-based equipment. However, large aisles are required to facilitate vehicle movement.

Ease of Installation Installation of an AGV system is relatively easy compared with conveyors or in-floor tow-lines. Also, if future expansion is required, an AGV is simpler and quicker to change. The AGV guidewire, embedded in the floor, carries the guidance signal which the vehicle senses as it follows the route. A guidance sensor on each vehicle detects the small electromagnetic field radiating from the guidepath wire and provides the vehicle with a reference to follow.

Labor Costs Both direct and indirect labor costs can be substantially reduced when an automated handling system is installed. Manually operated forklift trucks are eliminated; materials arrive at the workstations when they are required, eliminating waiting time and enabling the workers to spend more time being productive. An additional benefit of the improved material flow is the increased utilization of machinery, resulting from the elimination of waiting time.

AGVs cannot eliminate all of the manpower in a given area, but they can reduce it considerably. AGV systems can rarely, if ever, be justified by reduced labor costs alone.

Work Environment AGV systems provide improved working conditions, making the work in factories more pleasant for the people. Typically the AGV environment is cleaner, with better lighting and ventilation. It is quieter than other forms of automation, and the air is not contaminated with exhaust fumes from forklift trucks. AGVs can meet the strictest clean room standards, and also operate in hazardous environments unacceptable to humans such as welding and painting.

In assembly applications, the AGV can position the workpiece for the employee doing the work, enabling the worker to perform his task in the most comfortable position.

Quality In assembly applications AGVs have encouraged workers to improve the quality of the products through improved operator involvement. The workpiece is delivered to a stationary work area, so the assemblers don't have to work on a moving piece. This feature reduces worker fatigue. The vehicles can remain at an assembly station longer than scheduled should there be a problem. When the assemblers are satisfied with their work, they can release the vehicle to the next station. This feature minimizes mistakes and improves quality and craftsmanship.

Energy Costs An AGV requires less energy to operate than other forms of automation because it consumes power only when a vehicle must function. In addition, AGVs can operate with less lights, air conditioning, and heating.

Reduced Product Damage AGVs have reduced material damage caused by product handling, because the material handling system handles the product only when required—reducing the chances for damage. The products are handled with greater care, gently, and with controlled machine movements.

Inventory Control Computerized, automated material handling systems help to optimize and record the movement of materials. The AGV system can control the inventory in central storage, buffer storage, work-in-process, and material in transit. Managing the flow of materials means that the right materials arrive at the right place at the right time. This improved product flow eliminates materials left idle in storage areas and maintains storage areas at optimum inventory levels. By managing the flow of materials, the overall inventory and the number of inventory storage locations can be reduced. A rough guideline: inventory can be reduced between 8% to 12%.

Ergonomics The emphasis on ergonomics is sparked by more than a push for efficiency. These vehicles were developed to make jobs more rewarding. Workers in the AGV systems are being retrained to handle the more meaningful operations of this new material handling process. Instead of being the "doers," workers will be monitoring the automated systems and anticipating problems. The AGV systems will make workers more accountable, requiring them to be flexible, multi-functional, highly-skilled, and proactive rather than reactive.

Workers like AGVs and quickly adjust to them. The AGV technology is viewed by many companies as the correct approach for improving employee involvement in their work.

Integration Many automation systems are installed in an area of the factory to perform one function of a manufacturing operation. There can be several of these automated islands that are interdependent and require a connection. AGVs are one of the best ways to accomplish this task and make factories more suitable for automation. The vehicles can easily interface with other plant automation.

Figure 2.1 Mannesmann Demag AGV system using unit load vehicle to interface with an AS/RS. Unit load vehicles carry pallet loads into and out of the warehouse at a throughput rate of more than 200 pallets per hour. The guidepath length is more than 6000 feet. (Courtesy of Mannesmann Demag, Grand Rapids, Michigan)

2 CURRENT TYPES OF SYSTEMS

Automated guided vehicle systems use automatic material movement technology, which is becoming the most critical link in an automated factory. AGV use started in distribution and warehousing and expanded into the manufacturing arena. As the warehouse and factory areas become more automated and integrated, there is a demand for different types of AGV systems.

AGVs are being investigated and used to improve productivity, safety, and security; to better utilize floor space; to upgrade present material handling equipment; to enrich jobs; and more. Unlike conventional material handling systems, the AGV system offers more potential than its transportation role. It can be integrated into the manufacturing environment to make material delivery and part scheduling decisions, and to control a wide range of activities. These vehicles offer an extremely high level of efficiency, accuracy, versatility and tireless devotion to their tasks.

AGVs are ideally suited for automated non-synchronous transportation of material. The drive, load transfer, and buffer operations, controlled by the on-board and off-board control system, make AGVs suitable for warehousing, assembly operation, flexible manufacturing, and many other material handling applications. The primary use is to handle heavy and large loads, with flexible paths offering an alternative method for moving material. AGV systems have replaced conveyors, electric tow tractors, forklift trucks, and overhead cranes. These traditional material handling methods are primarily fixed-path and manually operated, providing large area coverage.

Automated material handling in many industries offers opportunities for increasing profits by reducing material handling costs. There has been substantial progress in developing AGVs for many different industries and applications, making this type of material handling more cost-effective than conventional methods. And AGVs are still evolving, becoming more versatile and dependable. Their acceptance in a diverse range of industry—aerospace, paper, automotive, pharmaceutical, textile, hospital, and food—proves that AGVs meet a variety of needs and have solved many different problems.

Typical guided vehicle applications include the following.

- Warehouses use AGVs to move incoming loads to storage points or to pickup stands for ASRS (automatic storage and retrieval system). AGVs also remove products from storage and move them to the shipping dock.

- Manufacturing companies use AGVs to move parts between machining centers.

- Prisons use AGVs to deliver meals.

- Industry and power plants use AGVs to handle hazardous waste.

- Hospitals use AGVs to move and deliver linen, medicines, and supplies.

- Textile mills use AGVs to handle spools of yarn.

- In storage yards, AGVs pick up and deliver heavy materials.

- In food processing plants, AGVs handle and stack food products in coolers and freezers.

- AGVs are used to supply piece parts to assembly lines.

- AGVs are used for paper roll handling in the newspaper printing industry and paper mills.

- In the automotive environment, AGV applications are numerous.

TYPICAL **AGV** APPLICATIONS

Four common AGV applications include AGV assembly systems, AGV warehouse systems, AGV use in flexible manufacturing systems, and AGV use in paper handling for the newspaper industry. Each of these applications incorporates different types of features in the vehicles and in the system control. A general overview of these applications follows.

AGV Assembly Systems

In these systems, the AGV carries large or small products that are assembled on the vehicle; the vehicle in many respects is a moving fixture to which parts are added in sequence until the product is complete. This concept is used in many new assembly plants because it emphasizes flexibility, productivity, quality, and teamwork.

The assembly AGV represents approximately 60% to 75% of the total number of AGVs in use today. The remaining vehicles are used in material delivery systems (forklift AGVs and unit load AGVs) and storage applications. The number of assembly AGVs is so large not because the number of assembly systems is large, but because each system requires many vehicles. It is difficult to set an average number of vehicles per system because each system is unique; the number can range from 500 to 20 vehicles per system.

Automated guided vehicle assembly systems were developed by the European automotive industry. American manufacturers accepted AGV assembly systems only recently, hesitating because this involved changing their assembly concepts and philosophy. The U.S. auto industry

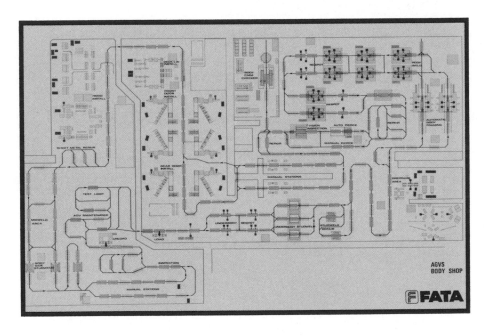

Figure 2.2 This system layout is for an automotive assembly plant. The system uses more than 100 AGVs to transport an automobile through the assembly process. The layout has more than 13,200 feet of guidepath and transports the automobile through the following operations: underbody robotic spot welding, robotic sealing systems, body side to underbody assembly, roof installation, piercing systems, and visual inspection systems. (Courtesy of FATA Automation, Livonia, Michigan)

has taken the lead over all other U.S. industries in the use of AGVs. General Motors uses hundreds of AGVs in assembly applications for engines, vehicle assembly, and vehicle trim.

These assembly vehicles are replacing the conveyor assembly lines in production environments. The disadvantage of conveyor material handling systems is that conveyors have a lot of moving parts; if one part fails, the complete assembly operation comes to a stop—usually a costly situation. Also, conveyors can interfere with the use of floor space, and are primarily hardware, which does not easily allow path changes to be made. All of these disadvantages are overcome with AGVs.

Figure 2.3 Different production intervals and many variations are typical for chassis assembly. In this newly designed production area, remaining welding, soldering, and grinding work is completed; hinges, lids and doors are installed. About 150 robot vehicles link 50 group workstations along a two-mile route. Upon accepting the body, the robot vehicle travels to the consignment station, picks up specific parts, and stops sequentially at the various workstations. Interim buffers separate the production section. During the entire production process the chassis remains on one vehicle. Attached parts are automatically called out along the travel route and delivered, synchronized with the body style. The entire system is controlled by an extensive computer network with subordinate process computer and program control. (Courtesy of Eisenmann Corporation, Crystal Lake, Illinois)

AGV assembly systems add flexibility to any manufacturing assembly process by allowing parallel operations to occur simultaneously, while establishing excellent management control. The greatest advantage of the system is that the assembly processes do not have to follow a set pattern, and there are few restrictions in laying out the individual work areas while maintaining a controlled manufacturing process. Moreover, the guidepath can be easily changed and the vehicle software can be reprogrammed. These assembly systems are integrated into the overall production environment, requiring computer control of the manufacturing process.

The AGV assembly system also enables manufacturers to offer the customer a greater variety of options or accessories through the flexibility of the assembly sequence. Most assemblies require considerable flexibility to change the product and make a family of models. This requirement can be easily handled by AGV assembly systems; unnecessary assembly steps can be eliminated, and the AGV can bypass unnecessary workstations. Such flexibility is not readily available with conventional conveyor assembly lines.

The AGVs are programmed according to the product and the options for the product each vehicle is carrying. The vehicle takes the product to the workstations required to assemble it. Depending on the variation being assembled, the AGV goes to only the assembly stations where components required for that model version are placed in the assembly.

A computer directs the vehicle to the workstations. The vehicles may queue up randomly in the assembly station, but they will exit in the correct build schedule sequence. This central control system makes it easier to re-route or re-assign various work processes on short notice. These systems also allow for individual tracking of items and measured work rates.

A typical assembly line using AGVs begins with the basic product; parts are added in sequence until the finished product has been built. For example, on an automotive assembly line an engine will be selected (for an auto body being assembled) and assembled in the sequence in which it will be used in the auto bodies. Once the engine is placed in the build schedule, it will emerge in sequence even though it

Figure 2.4 Roberts' TrakStar Model RTA-105, uni-directional unit load vehicle, equipped with an electro-mechanical lift. The operator installs a few parts before the vehicle progresses to the next station. (Courtesy of Roberts Corporation, Lansing, Michigan)

will take different paths through the assembly stations. With the AGV assembly systems it is possible to break the product sequence if assembly or manufacturing equipment breaks down; the vehicle can avoid the inoperable workstation, move to the next station, and return to the inoperable workstation after it has been repaired.

The vehicle transports the assembly to a workstation. As the vehicle comes to a stop, two to four workers gather around the vehicle and begin to install parts or do the entire assembly job. Assembly time is between 2 and 20 minutes. The vehicle then advances through each station until the product has been completely assembled.

The vehicle is programmed to move on after a predetermined assembly time, but if there is any problem, a member of the team can press a button and hold the vehicle until everything is completed. The team decides when the entire assembly is complete and when quality standards are met, then releases the assembly back into the system. Workers are not driven by production time; they are allowed to take extra time when it is required.

The finished products are unloaded from the AGV by robots, by automatic transfer stations, manually, or by the AGVs themselves. The AGV then returns to the beginning of the assembly system.

Another advantage of this assembly process is that defective parts are spotted early, and necessary repairs can be made in a workstation instead of down line; thus the assemblies are produced with a higher level of quality. Assemblies with special problems can be sent to rework areas to be corrected.

Battery charging on assembly vehicles is done while the vehicle is in the workstation, or while the vehicle is waiting to enter a workstation. Electrical contacts on the bottom of the AGVs connect with electrical contacts in the floor, and the batteries are charged as the vehicles wait. There is no separate charging area required in the system, and because battery charge condition is monitored by each vehicle's microprocessor, the vehicles require no regular battery service.

Operator interfaces to AGVs are important, particularly in assembly systems. Operators want to work at a comfortable level that gives them easy access to the assembly, with sufficient room on all sides. The power lifts on the vehicles allow the workpiece to be raised, lowered, and tilted to ensure that each assembler can work at the most convenient height so the work can be quickly done. Before the AGV gets to a workstation it automatically positions the product to the proper elevation. If the operator wants to further adjust the work height, he can use the manual control to do it. This feature eliminates heavy and dirty work through automatic solutions and makes it possible for males and females to do any kind of work.

AGV assembly systems create a new working environment in areas requiring a high concentration of personnel. The environment is quieter than that of conventional assembly systems. Also, AGV systems eliminate exposed floor rails, greasy conveyor chains, and overhead conveyors. Because there are few pieces of fixed equipment, the work area is more open, providing better light intensity, improved ventilation, and better housekeeping.

In these systems people work together as teams, which helps motivate the workers and increases morale—measurable by fewer unexcused absences. With all the advantages of the non-synchronous AGV assembly system and the multi-team assembly technique, an assembly line can operate without every person being in place, provided one complete team is in position. The team can vary its rate of work during the day and take short breaks without affecting production.

The daily output using AGV assembly systems is close to 100% of scheduled production regardless of disturbances, problems with absenteeism, and delay caused by training of new employees. This is possible because of the flexibility of the system. The system has great recovery capability; if the line must slow down for any reason, the slack can be made up easily compared to the conventional assembly line. For example, if a system is disrupted due to the failure of one vehicle or one workstation, only the 1/nth part of the transport capacity or workstation capacity is affected. The system itself continues to operate. People working in this type of environment like it more and produce more, and the quality of the product increases. These factors will gain more significance in the future because they minimize production losses.

AGV assembly systems permit manufacturers to maintain a flexible staffing policy. If demand for the product decreases, the production rate can be adjusted by reducing the number of assembly teams or by allowing different teams to work odd or even days, giving everyone part-time work—generally a more acceptable alternative than shutting down the entire plant.

In addition, there are advantages in the way maintenance can be performed. Preventive maintenance can be scheduled according to production flow and performed at lower cost. If an individual vehicle fails, it can be pushed off the line without disturbing the flow. After the vehicle is repaired, it can be returned to the guidepath.

AGV assembly systems also enhance the use of automation and enable operators to carry out tasks which in the past were either technically or economically not feasible for automation—such as assembly work that interfaces with robots. Since the work remains stationary during assembly it is much easier for all types of robots to be used in the assembly operation. Robots have been difficult to apply in the past because of the continuous moving nature of the assembly line. Furthermore, robots can now do the tedious and unpleasant chores that automotive workers dislike.

In general, AGV equipment is initially more expensive than conventional assembly equipment. However, after all the advantages are considered, AGVs are more efficient and more cost-effective than conventional assembly lines.

AGV Warehouse Systems

Automated guided vehicles are a popular means of transportation in warehousing operations. The first AGVs were used in warehousing; since their origination they have undergone considerable changes. AGVs have become more standardized, making them less expensive and easier to install. Furthermore, they have become a tough competitor and major threat to the conventional forklift truck manufacturers.

Warehouses that use automatic storage and retrieval systems (ASRS) to store pallets are enhancing their systems with AGVs. The major material handling consideration in these operations, where the volume is high and automatic

Figure 2.5 AGVs interface with a high-rise storage system, achieving a throughput rate of more than 600 units per day. (Courtesy of Eaton-Kenway, Salt Lake City, Utah)

load transfer occurs, is the horizontal transportation of pallets to and from the warehouse, to other areas in the manufacturing plant, between the pickup and delivery (P&D) stations, and to individual storage positions. AGVs provide an efficient and economical method for transporting material throughout the operation.

The number of load configurations being stored in an ASRS has increased in the past few years; this has led to different styles of guided vehicles. The wide range of features available on AGVs has enabled the ASRS to remain competitive and flexible in material handling.

Most AGV systems that are computer-controlled can easily interface with an automatic storage and retrieval system. The central computer automatically tracks and holds the status of every loaded pallet in the warehouse and material handling system and directs the vehicles in coordination with the loads moving into and out of the warehouse.

Figure 2.6 Control Engineering Company Prontow Auto-Trans unit load vehicle with automatic lift/lower deck. This vehicle transports pallet loads throughout a distribution center. Note that not all loads are strapped to the pallet. (Courtesy of Control Engineering Company, Harbor Springs, Michigan)

The AGV that interfaces with the ASRS is typically a bi-directional vehicle with a six- to eight-inch powered lift for load transfer. The vehicle drives into the P&D area, stopping next to a loaded P&D station; the pallet is then transferred to the vehicle's supporting table. In another common load transfer method, the vehicle making a pickup drives beneath the load stand, stopping under the loaded pallet. The lift in the AGV activates and lifts the pallet clear of the stand. To complete the pickup, the vehicle returns to the main guidepath while lowering the pallet onto the AGV supporting table. The vehicle then delivers the pallet to a station in another part of the plant or warehouse as instructed by the central computer. For pallets being returned to the warehouse, the AGV transports the pallet to the end of the ASR aisle, raises the loaded pallet, drives beneath the load stand, lowers the lift, positions the pallet securely on the load stand, and drives away.

In a warehousing application companies have discovered that AGVs:

- Can be arranged to simultaneously meet the needs of both warehousing and manufacturing applications using the same type of vehicles.

- Provide continuous operation at optimum speeds with minimal interface with people.

- Deliver loads to destinations great distances away from the central warehouse.

FMS-Flexible Manufacturing System

Almost every flexible manufacturing system (FMS) is a major engineering accomplishment. These systems represent the leading edge of technology in machine tools, material handling systems, and manufacturing know-how, integrating computer controls, programmable controllers, automatic transfer devices, robots, AGVs, and sensors in one system. The key components common to every FMS include machine centers, wash stations, de-burr equipment, inspection equipment, and chip containers.

FMS increases the utilization of machine tools and reduces the work-in-process time. The typical workpiece, in the traditional factory, spends approximately 5% of its factory time being manufactured into a good part; the remaining time the part is being transported, waiting for mating parts, or waiting to be worked on. When the part is being worked on, it may wait for a machine to be set up, which means the part may actually be worked on only 2% or 3% of the time. Use of FMS improves the situation.

Flexible manufacturing systems arrange several re-programmable machine tools into cells that perform related work on manufactured products. These cells are connected by an automated material handling transport system, with the complete process being controlled by a computer. The best approach is to install a flexible manufacturing system that makes an entire product; however, few such systems exist.

The major reason for the relatively slow growth of FMS in the United States is expense; management is concerned about the slow payback. Acceptable payback periods in the U.S. are typically two to three years—a range that is inappropriate for justifying FMS investments. The longer operating life and flexibility suggest allowing a longer payback period.

Flexible manufacturing systems are essential if manufacturers plan to use two other advanced manufacturing tech-

Figure 2.7 Control Engineering Company Auto-Trans vehicle used in a FMS application. Vehicle automatically transports and exchanges high tolerance machining pallets. (Courtesy of Control Engineering Company, Harbor Springs, Michigan)

nologies: just-in-time and computer-integrated manufacturing. FMS embraces these two manufacturing technologies, produces higher product quality, and enables manufacturers to react faster to market demands. Furthermore, it is possible to cut the lead time of finished parts from days to hours. This concept will reduce the "lot size" of a production run and, therefore, further reduce inventory.

The key to flexible manufacturing is that the system must be able to make the same product in different sizes or styles without being shut down. In the FMS environment the manufacturing process takes on a broad scope of operation. Effectively, raw materials are entered into one end of the manufacturing system and finished parts emerge from the other end. The systems should be able to produce one

Figure 2.8 Murata Robo Carrier Model RC-500 transports parts and fixtures in machining centers. Vehicle has a capacity of 11,000 pounds. Vehicle uses a wire guidance system, is equipped with front and rear wheel steering, and can travel in all directions: forward, reverse, sideways. (Courtesy of Murata of America, Troy, Michigan)

part as economically as 100 parts, because the set-up times have been reduced to zero.

All successful flexible manufacturing systems have a common characteristic—each system component will enhance and be enhanced by other system components, from fixtures to the central computer, from chip conveyor to robot, from carbide insert to machine tool. The FMS user must think of the system in its entirety as opposed to the individual machines.

A basic automation feature in a flexible manufacturing system is the unattended machining system. Ideally, no operator intervention is desired. Making the unmanned machining center work means replacing the operator with automated monitoring and servicing of the system. An entire FMS line can require only two to four operators, depending on the number of machine tools in operation and the throughput requirements of the system. It is desired to operate each machine without an operator for prolonged periods of time. To achieve the longer machinery uptime, it is often necessary to reduce the feeds and speeds or add

Figure 2.9 Unit load vehicle used in machine tool application. Extractor wheels are used to power off-board conveyors. The fixed pallet is loaded by a Puma Robot. (Courtesy of Apogee Robotics, Fort Collins, Colorado)

machining cycles to preserve tool life. The typical machine tool utilization rates are 60% to 75%.

Integrating the FMS with the proper type of material handling system is a major consideration. If routing flexibility is limited by a synchronous material handling system, parts will be machined according to the order in which they entered the system. This can severely constrain the flexibility in configuring the FMS for different production runs. The optimum material handling system is one that handles a variety of parts in random order, can be re-programmed to handle new parts and new routings, and also handles a well-defined family of parts in a pre-determined sequence.

AGVs fulfill these requirements. They have proven their versatility and adaptability. The material handling system transports the workpiece from station to station. AGVs can be mechanically adapted to carry machine pallets, tool magazines, and chip containers. They position pallets accurately and directly alongside the machine tool interface. This enables the pallet to be transferred cleanly, running on aligned guideways or similar devices. The workpiece is transported on a machined pallet, fixture base, or other interface units so that work-machine registration is accurate, rapid, and automatic, even when the sequence is random. The part usually doesn't have to be re-fixtured unless the mounting side of the part requires machining. Basically, this means any machine tool available can be used for any purpose in any sequence.

The control system of the FMS consists of three computers to control parts handling and the machine tools. These computers include the host computer, material handling computer, and the machining centers computer (CNC-computer numerical control).

The host computer controls the entire FMS operation. Communication lines are established between the host computer, the CNCs, and the material handling computer. The host computer directs the material handling computer for part movement throughout the system. After the part has reached its destination, the host computer communicates with the CNC, directing it to move the pallet from the input queue onto the machining surface. As the pallet is being moved onto the machining surface, the host computer further communicates with the CNC, passing down from its database the part program and tool setup. At the conclusion of the machining process, the CNC indicates the completion of the operation to the host computer. The host computer then directs the CNC to move the pallet from the machine table to the output queue.

The second computer in the FMS is the material handling computer, which controls movement of each part throughout the entire manufacturing process. This computer is responsible for moving the pallet from station to station, continuously monitoring and memorizing all pallet locations within the work-in-process, along with the status (full or empty) and, if necessary, the reference number of each load held.

A typical FMS station will have a machine tool, P&D station, or chip removal station. Each station has three or more possible pallet locations—the workstation, the input queue, and the output queue. Parts on the input queue are ready to be machined at that station. This queue establishes a small buffer storage for the machining center, providing additional work part storage. Parts on the output queue have already been machined and are waiting to be relocated. Servicing the machine cell is an AGV to provide immediate response and flexibility for the entire system.

Workpieces enter the FMS at the sizing and qualifying station, where the parts and fixtures are checked to make sure the parts are mounted correctly and the part and fixture are within the size limits. From this point a workpiece may proceed anywhere within the system, depending on which workstation and operation the host computer selects. The workpieces are returned to the sizing and qualifying station for repositioning parts on the fixture and taking finished parts out of the system.

A successful FMS should operate unattended. To accomplish this, the manufacturing system must be pre-loaded. Considerable effort will be expended to pre-load the system during the first shift of operation, with reduced or no manpower for the second and third shifts. Normally this work-in-process storage for part pallets, empty pallets, and fixtures is an integral part of the FMS cell.

AGVs can play an important role in integrating the material handling system with the work-in-process storage. The forklift vehicle with a mast and load transfer table can move loads in and out of remote storage areas. The vehicles will deliver the loads and place them in rack storage, two, three, or four levels high, and retrieve the loads from the rack to deliver them to the required machining center. This in-process storage saves premium factory floor space by storing the pallets in the vertical rack rather than on the floor.

As the popularity of FMS increases, the AGV will become more important to the overall success of the FMS. AGVs meet the system's demand for flexibility, reduce risk of obsolescence, and increase the system's useful life.

Paper Handling System

AGVs are used increasingly in commercial printing and the newspaper industry. The production processes are different, but material handling is similar; both industries need to handle waste paper material, transport paper rolls into and out of a warehouse, and handle palletized materials.

Newspapers have turned to AGVs for two reasons. First, intense competition demands that large printers cut production costs and reduce waste. Second, a newspaper's entire operation is time-dependent, with no room for equipment breakdowns. Each day a different paper must be written, produced, and distributed, and every piece of equipment must function reliably and "just-in-time." The material handling system is a vital link in this production process—and AGVs enable newspapers to cut costs while increasing flexibility and reliability.

The material handling system performs the critical task of feeding paper rolls into the presses. The rolls must be transported from the warehouse, stripped of their outer wrappers, moved to the lay-down area for in-process storage (to cover peak consumption needs), and then transported to the press. In just one hour this process can occur 60 to 70 times.

Newspapers have moved paper rolls primarily with forklifts, in-floor tow-lines, push carts, pallet jacks, and overhead cranes. Numerous people are required to assist in and oversee these operations. The systems are dependable; more people can always be added to get the job done. But these systems also produce a lot of waste and are expensive.

In a typical newspaper AGV application, the paper rolls are 48 to 54 inches in diameter and weigh more than 1000 pounds. The rolls are received from the truck dock and brought to the warehouse using forklift trucks. Forklifts or overhead cranes store the rolls vertically.

Forklift trucks, conveyors, or AGVs take the paper rolls from the warehouse to the stripping station, where the outer protective paper and any damaged paper is removed. AGVs generally handle all transportation from this point on. During slack periods the vehicles pick up rolls and move them to the lay-down area, building up inventory. During

Figure 2.10 This FMC Model FV-40/80 fork type vehicle handles paper rolls in the press room of a newspaper. The paper rolls are delivered from the warehousing area to the individual positioning stands at each press. This is part of a ten-vehicle system which delivers rolls to 22 press locations. The system is sized to handle a throughput of 75 rolls per hour. System control handles all roll inventory and roll management. The system controller is a DEC 11/73 with hot backup. (Courtesy of FMC Corporation, Material Handling Systems Division, Chalfont, Pennsylvania)

peak periods they move the rolls from the lay-down area to the printing presses.

When a press operator needs a particular type of roll, he activates a call button to request a prepared paper roll. This roll is delivered from the lay-down area to a floor stand next to the press, where an operator manually inserts the roll. In some cases the vehicle delivers the paper rolls to an automatic press loader.

AGVs also are used in the binding and inserting area, where palletized loads must be moved from the presses to the binding machinery and then to storage. These pallets are normally moved from floor to floor, or rack to rack, so a pallet jack or fork vehicle can be used.

Figure 2.11 This vehicle handles 3000-pound rolls of newsprint measuring 50 inches by 55 inches. The AGV automatically places the paper rolls into rack storage and retrieves them when required by the presses. Vehicle in this photo is loading a paper roll queuing area. (Courtesy of FMC Corporation, Material Handling Systems Division, Chalfont, Pennsylvania)

Typical System Components The following components are found in most paper handling systems:

- **Vehicle** AGVs can accurately position the paper rolls, eliminating the need for positioning devices and other handling equipment. Furthermore, the fork vehicle can be designed to handle the paper rolls, and to both handle and transport waste containers between the production areas and the scales and waste paper bailers. The forks are designed to cradle paper rolls and handle pallets. They are beveled to minimize contact pressure between the fork and the paper roll, minimizing damage to the paper. The fork can also be designed with a flat top so the vehicles can be used to transport pallets. The fork vehicle can be either a counterbalanced vehicle or a straddle vehicle. The counterbalanced vehicle uses much smaller aisles, can maneuver in tight areas, and is less expensive.

- **Redundant Controls** As earlier explained, the importance of the material handling system cannot be understated—the system must operate to produce newspapers efficiently. To avoid the possibility of the system going down because of control hardware, control hardware is redundantly configured; two computer control systems are available to operate the material handling system. If one system goes down for any reason, the second computer will operate the system until the first is repaired.

- **Host Computer Interface** The AGV system is frequently interfaced with the company's host computer. The combined system (host plus AGV control) can monitor the paper rolls used in each press and the total number of rolls used from the inventory, maintaining accurate inventory records and providing management reports on the performance of the entire operation. This information can be used in managing a future press run.

System Benefits AGVs used to transport paper rolls can be compared to the method found in most newspaper companies—the tow-chain system, in which carts are towed around the perimeter of the press room, carrying rolls that are removed as needed. The carts roll on the floor, with the tow chain recessed in the floor. The benefits of an AGV system over a tow-chain system are:

- **Inventory Control and Performance Statistics** The AGV system can maintain the inventory of paper rolls and coordinate it with the production of newspapers. In addition, performance statistics can be obtained for the AGV material handling system, the production of newspapers, paper waste, and most other vital areas related to the material handing system.

- **System Reliability** In the event of a component or control failure, most AGV systems can continue to operate. If a component fails on a vehicle, there are other vehicles in the system to continue the transportation of paper rolls to the press. If a control fails, most AGV systems have a redundant computer system to continue the material operation while the failed hardware is being repaired.

- **Batch Control** If the production manager wants to run a specific batch of paper from a specific vendor, it requires considerable effort using the traditional tow-line system. With an AGV system, however, vendor paper rolls can be delivered to any designated printing press. This is frequently required when a new vendor's paper is being tested for its ability to run on the printing presses.

- **Reduced Paper Roll Damage** Paper that is torn, creased, or damaged cannot be run through the press. If the paper roll is damaged in transportation and handling, the damaged paper must be stripped from the roll. The AGV material handling process reduces the amount of wasted paper because the vehicle handles paper rolls gently. AGVs can reduce the waste incurred with tow-chains and even forklift trucks.

- **Safety** Safety is another benefit of using AGVs for this application. Because there are fewer mechanisms in the handling process, and fewer people involved, there are fewer hazards. That reduces the number of employee accidents and worker's compensation claims.

- **Manpower Savings** Fewer people are required in the material handling operation. This saving occurs due to the reduced number of forklift trucks in the operation, and the reduced number of people required to support a tow-line system.

- **Utilities Costs** AGVs consume far less electrical energy than the traditional tow-chain system, reducing electrical costs.

- **System Expansion** The AGV system is easier and cheaper to expand because no building modifications are required. In most cases, the guidepath has to be expanded and the guidepath map (in the system control or vehicle control) has to be re-programmed; this can be done in a few days. With the tow-line system, the floor has to be recessed for the tow-chain and the tow-chain system has to be expanded, an expensive and time-consuming process.

AGV System Categories[1]

Investment in AGV technology will not necessarily guarantee success, and the choice of incorrect AGV technologies for a specific application can have lasting consequences, binding a company to a material handling system that may take years to undo—thus the importance of selecting the proper AGV system category. In all cases one must use AGVs realistically. Some applications will benefit from AGVs while others may show only marginal improvement. Using AGVs in the wrong application may reduce companies' flexibility with only marginal improvements.

The starting point in selecting the correct system category is to match the application requirements, future requirements, level of intelligence, and sophistication with the system category. It's important to pay particular attention to the vehicle dispatch methods, system controls, utilization of vehicles, and flexibility required now and in the future.

The simplest category is a manually operated system; as the application requirements grow, the level of system intelligence and vehicle control must be increased. Each category has its own optimum point where the system operates most effectively. The best category for an application depends on several variables, including type of communication, type of vehicle selected, guidepath length, number of vehicles, number of pickup and delivery stations, type of anti-collision system, and volume of material to be handled.

To simplify AGV selection, the above variables are classified into three general control categories: Category 1, the standard system with basic control; Category 2, the advanced system with microprocessor controls; and Category 3, the fully automated material handling system with a central computer control system that may interface with a host computer. In the first and second system categories, humans play an important role in the control functions; in the third system category, humans only supervise and troubleshoot the system functions. It is important to understand the type of functions performed by each category of system.

Category 1: Standard System with Basic Controls

Category 1 systems are stand-alone material handling systems; they are used only for material handling. Generally these are low-cost systems providing simple destination-to-destination transportation with low throughput requirements. There are usually one to four vehicles used in Category 1 systems. The AGV is simply a load carrier, the simplest type available, with very little on-board intelligence and capability. These vehicles are referred to as "dumb vehicles" because they lack sophisticated on-board controls.

The typical guidepath is one continuous loop, with "forward sensing" blocking to prevent vehicle collisions. These systems require no off-board controllers, no central computer systems for vehicle scheduling or generating performance reports, no real-time monitors, and no capability for tracking vehicles in transit. Vehicles are recognized only when they are stationary at a P&D stand or queuing area. These systems are the cheapest to install.

Vehicle dispatching for Category 1 systems requires people to direct the vehicles; there are two methods.

On-Board Dispatch The on-board dispatch system requires the destination address instructions to be manually entered directly into the selector keypad on the vehicle. The on-board microprocessor then directs the vehicle to its destination. When the vehicle arrives at its destination, it may automatically unload, or more typically for this type of application, an operator boards the vehicle, positions it, and deposits the load. The vehicle remains wherever it has completed its last assignment. When the vehicle is required for another assignment, the person at the last station sends it to the required station.

This is the most basic form of system management and is the most flexible because of extensive human interface.

Off-Board Call System In off-board call systems, the vehicles lodge at one location until needed. Workers enter requests for vehicles at the workstation's stationary call box, which is wired to a floor sensor. When a request is entered, the sensor is activated and a vehicle is released along the guidepath. It travels until the activated sensor stops the vehicle. If the call request is cancelled, the vehicle won't stop; instead, it proceeds to its next call request.

Some of these system do not direct the vehicle to a specific location; the vehicles simply travel until they find a station that needs servicing. The disadvantage to this type of system is that the last station on the guidepath may not receive proper servicing. To overcome this disadvantage, call systems can be made to call a specific vehicle to a specific location.

In both dispatch methods, the disadvantage of involving people in the positioning, loading and unloading of the vehicles is that it can slow down the complete system if people are not immediately available when the vehicle arrives at the workstation. The vehicle must not be used for buffer storage for products it is carrying. For these reasons a Category 1 system should not be used in material handling systems requiring a high system efficiency or a high throughput capacity.

Summary of Category 1 Systems Category 1 systems have specific advantages: initial low cost, ease of managing the system, and controls that are easily understood by maintenance personnel.

There are also disadvantages. The system is not easily upgradeable, it is difficult to interface with other control systems, material is not delivered efficiently, the material handling operation is operator-intensive with a low level of automation, and system throughput capacity is low. The time in which call requests are handled depends on the actual length of guidepath routing, the number of call requests at a given time, and the number of vehicles in the system. Because of this slow response time, sufficient queueing of product is required at each pickup and delivery point.

Category 2: Advanced System with Microprocessor Controls

Category 2 systems are also stand-alone material handling systems, used only for material handling. These systems provide more flexibility, improved response time, increased automation, and generally more capabilities.

The guidepath for this type of system is not a continuous loop, but instead is more complex. There are secondary guidepath routes, commonly called spurs or branches, off the main guidepath route, commonly referred to as a trunk. Also, there are intersections, vehicle queues, and multiple pickup and drop-off locations. The complex guidepath offers increased flexibility: complicated networks of material flow offer alternative routes for each vehicle to follow to each P&D station. Depending on the size of the area covered by the guidepath, the typical Category 2 system may require five to fifteen vehicles; however, the more AGVs, the more complicated the system and the more system monitoring required.

A Category 2 vehicle offers several improvements over a Category 1 vehicle. An important feature is the vehicle's capability for automatic load transfer at the workstations and remote programming of individual vehicles. There are more sophisticated controls aboard the vehicles, and traffic controls provide guidepath blocking. Both the control costs and the vehicle costs are higher than those of a Category 1 vehicle.

A significant difference between Category 1 and Category 2 systems is that in Category 2 systems, instructions are communicated to the AGVs automatically. The vehicle can both receive and transmit data to the system controllers, eliminating the need for extensive operator interface with the vehicles. Depending on the application requirements and the communication method selected, the vehicle can receive the data while traveling, or while stationary. The types of communication used include inductive ground loops, infrared, and radio transmission. These forms of communication will be discussed in detail later in this book.

In these systems a programmable logic controller (PLC) or a microprocessor handles the system control. The system bases its decisions on the status of the various input signals, processes call requests, and then directs the vehicles automatically according to the specified vehicle blocking rules, vehicle selection rules, and route selection rules. Inventory control and load tracking from station to station are also available with this control category.

A central console in these systems provides centralized control, vehicle tracking, and vehicle management. An operator, serving as a central dispatcher, uses the console to monitor all pickup and delivery requests and the system. The centralized controller then files the transaction requests, prioritizes them if required, dispatches vehicles to selected storage locations to automatically pick up loads, and then dispatches the loaded vehicles to their final destination. This control system still requires an operator who can see the vehicles in addition to monitoring a CRT display. These systems are used when the application can't justify a totally computer-controlled system.

In Category 2 systems, vehicles are dispatched from one or more queues using a remote dispatch technique. When a call request is given, the centralized controller releases a vehicle from the closest queue. After finishing the request the vehicle is either assigned another call request or returned to the closest queue. Calls are thus responded to more quickly than in Category 1 call dispatch systems.

Category 3: Central Computer Control System with Interface to Other Systems

Category 3 systems are integrated material handling systems. They are integrated into other manufacturing systems and do more than just transport materials. The Category 3 systems provide the highest level of control over the system and the vehicles. These systems are complex because they do all operations and material movements automatically, providing real-time status, obtaining the highest utilization of vehicles, insuring maximum flexibility, providing optimum system throughput, and permitting automatic tracking of every load in the system. Where throughput volume is high and automatic load transfer occurs, the Category 3 system is very efficient.

These systems eliminate the need for the central dispatcher by replacing that person with a computer control. The computer control provides complete vehicle and system coordination. The vehicles respond to a system management controller's commands for carrying out work assignments. In these systems people are not used to enter information in the computer system or move the work-in-process. The lack of human interface eliminates the risk of any improper information being entered into the central computer. The AGV computer control system controls and monitors the movement of all loads at all times.

This control system can interface with other systems (robots, conveyors, automatic storage and retrieval systems). The AGV computer control system communicates through a serial link or data highway with a PLC, a microprocessor, or a combination of the two within the AGV system to provide real-time control. When the system or a vehicle is interrupted, the real-time control provides a faster reaction to the interruption. Real-time control reduces the time lag for information updating, speeds response to production demands of the AGV system, and increases accuracy of work-in-process inventory. The AGV computer control system can also be linked to a host computer, which monitors inventory and process control functions for the entire plant. This increased complexity in the system requires more sophisticated controls, more engineering, more software, and more system planning.

The key element of control for this level of system is the identification of the vehicle's position in relation to a specific location, and the management of vehicle traffic and material movement. Total system monitoring allows communication updates and high response levels to material movement requests. Vehicles' identification, position, destination, and condition (loaded or unloaded) provide the controller with a constant update of the system status. The controller can then select an appropriate vehicle for a work assignment.

An automatic call by a load-present condition at a pickup location is incorporated in these systems. The calls can be routed to the central controller, through local area networking, and logged in for sequential release. Each call is responded to on a first-in first-out basis (FIFO). The first call received is communicated to the first vehicle in the queue. This means tasks are assigned to the vehicles in an orderly fashion and insures that all call locations are responded to equally.

Typically the guidepath network is much more complex, with multiple intersections (convergence, divergence), multiple pickup or drop-off stations, and a number of vehicles interacting throughout the system.

The number of vehicles in these systems depends on the size, sophistication, and vendor philosophy of computer controls. Systems have been designed to control hundreds of vehicles but the typical number of vehicles is 12 to 60.

The flexibility of these systems is also unlimited. The system is dynamic, allowing the central controller to remain in control of all significant events, and leaving room for material movement decisions to the last moment. This can be of particular importance when the host computer is responsible for controlling multiple functions and other material handling products (robots, conveyors, automatic storage and retrieval systems) within the facility.

These systems are expensive compared to Category 2 systems. The major areas of increased cost are in the control hardware and software, and all other automation within the system. The vehicle and guidepath installation costs do not increase dramatically over those of the Category 2 system.

Summary

The three general categories of AGV systems have been reviewed, looking at call requests and dispatching of vehicles. There is some overlap in each category in terms of system effectiveness and vehicle utilization, but a big difference in flexibility and throughput capability. Each plan to develop an AGV system should identify the requirements for load movements, accessibility of all call locations, and the speed at which the vehicles should respond to these call requests. In some simple applications, a Category 1 control will work appropriately. If more material movement is required, Category 2 control is more applicable. High throughput, multiple stations, and complex guidepath networking requiring a sophisticated level of automation require a Category 3 control to insure a dynamic system operation and high utilization of the vehicles and system.

REFERENCES

1) "AGV System Categories" is based in part on: Robert D. Rienecke, "AGVS Call /Dispatch Systems," AGVS Proceeding 1985, p. 75, The Material Handling Institute, Charlotte, North Carolina.

Figure 3.1 This is a family of AGVs manufactured by FATA. (Courtesy of FATA Automation, Livonia, Michigan)

3 THE PROPER VEHICLE

Once the preliminary requirements of the material handling system are defined, including the type of system category, it is time to consider what type of vehicle best suits the application. The success of the entire AGV system depends on choosing the correct vehicle and system control category; both must be right for a successful system. The type of AGV is critical; the wrong choice can have lasting consequences.

AGVs come in a broad range of capabilities, and the characteristics vary widely from application to application. Factors to consider when choosing the vehicle include what type of system control category will be used, what equipment the AGV must be able to interface with, what type of products are to be transported, and whether any special maneuvering of the loads is required.

AGVs are designed to interface with robots, automatic storage and retrieval systems (ASRS), parts carousels, and conveyors, and to link islands of automation. To enhance the interface between the AGV and the other material handling equipment, AGVs can be equipped with shuttle arms, robots, clamping devices, and other positioning equipment—thus their increased popularity in computer integrated manufacturing (CIM).

AGVs have four common characteristics: they require no driver, they are usually battery powered, they are automatically guided, and they have a communication method to receive and transmit information. Other attributes include:

- Load adaptors
- Type of load transfer mechanism
- Maximum load capacity
- Payload type and size
- Vehicle size
- Maneuverability
- Automatic loading and unloading
- Steering configuration
- Number of drive wheels
- Drive directions: forward, reverse, sideways
- Suspension
- Type of guidepath: wire, chemical, optical, and 3D paths
- Towing capability

The functions of any vehicle can be broken down into the movements required for load positioning and transportation. The movements include:

Floor Position to Floor Position Movement This movement is picking up a load from the floor and delivering the load to another floor position at another location within the system.

Floor Position to Elevated Position Movement This movement is picking up a load at the floor position and moving it to an elevated position, or picking up a load from an elevated position and moving it to a floor position. This movement occurs in storing and retrieving loads from a rack.

Elevated Position Movement to Elevated Position Movement This movement typically occurs when transferring a load from load stand to load stand.

Transportation Movement Horizontal transportation is accomplished by all vehicles. What differs from vehicle to vehicle is the ability to travel forward, in reverse, and sideways. Multiple horizontal movements also may not be available with all types of vehicles.

TYPES OF VEHICLES

There are many types of vehicles currently available, differing primarily in the purpose for which they are designed. The six major AGV classifications include:

- Driverless train. These vehicles are also referred to as tuggers or tow vehicles.

- Pallet vehicles, also referred to as walkie's and pallet jack vehicles.

- Unit load vehicles, flat bed vehicles, load transports.

- Fork-type vehicles: conventional vehicles, straddle vehicles, high lift vehicles, and side loading vehicles.

- Lightweight unit load vehicles and module transport vehicles.

- Special vehicles including assembly vehicles.

The first five classifications are considered standard by many vendors. These standardized vehicles have been designed for a broad range of applications and therefore have some limitations compared to a vehicle designed for a specific application. These limitations have to be evaluated against the advantages in short delivery time, lower price, and proven reliability of the vehicle and its components.

The last classification is the special vehicle used for assembly applications and applications where a standard vehicle cannot be used. The primary disadvantages of the special vehicle are the cost of the engineering design and the lack of a proven vehicle.

Driverless Trains

The driverless train is used for material delivery applications. This type of vehicle consists of a tractor that tows two to five trailers. The material is loaded onto a series of trailers for delivery throughout a plant. These systems are generally used where material volumes are heavy and material is moved at least 500 feet between pickup and delivery.

During a trip around the guidepath, the towing tractor makes several stops at predetermined stations. At each stop, loads are added or removed from the trailers, or the trailers are uncoupled. Since each towing tractor can move several pallet loads at once, this method is usually justified by the elimination of forklift trucks and operators.

Figure 3.2 Control Engineering Company Prontow Model 602 driverless vehicle used in a newspaper company for transferring paper rolls from the warehouse to the press room. (Courtesy of Control Engineering Company, Harbor Springs, Michigan)

Figure 3.3 Caterpillar's Self-Guided Towing Vehicle, Model SGT, can pick up, move, and drop off trailers with a total gross weight of 18,000 pounds. Vehicle is best suited to high throughput, long distance applications. Free-ranging vehicle uses low power laser scanning of bar code targets combined with advanced dead reckoning techniques to navigate. No buried wires or stripes on the floor are needed. (Courtesy of Caterpillar Industrial, Mentor, Ohio)

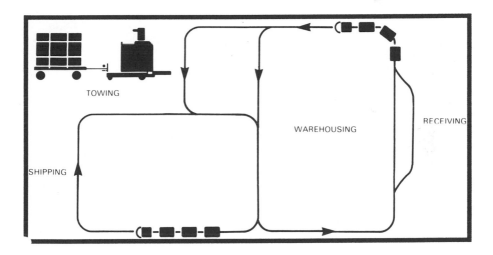

Figure 3.4 Guidepath layout for a driverless train application. (Courtesy of Gary Koff, Mannesmann Demag, Grand Rapids, Michigan)

Figure 3.5 Demag/Barrett Model 24TEB tractor is used to tow carts in the transportation of materials from receiving and packaging locations to the warehouse and to shipping as needed. Each vehicle is capable of towing three trailers. The guidepath length is 9,300 feet. (Courtesy of Mannesmann Demag, Grand Rapids, Michigan)

Driverless trains can be manually driven off the guide-path, increasing the flexibility of the equipment by enabling the train to service remote destinations. When the train is under manual control and leaves the guidepath, it can no longer be controlled or monitored by the control system.

Tractor AGV speeds are 200-275 feet per minute, providing tractive effort up to several tones. Rolling load resistance of the towed trailers is 2% of their total weight. The tractors can handle slight grades. Driverless tractors can pull trailer loads of 8000 to 50,000 pounds. Space requirements for driverless trains depend on the number of trailers being towed, and the type of steering on the trailer. The minimum radius of bends is approximately six to seven feet.

These vehicles operate in the textiles industry, paper industry, rubber industry, general manufacturing, and warehousing. In a warehousing application, the towing tractors are loaded in the warehouse and pull a train of supplies around the plant, distributing them to various workstations. Driverless trains are a good way to handle awkward size loads.

Manual loading of materials on the trailers is common; heavy loads are handled by manually-operated forklift trucks, which generally travel less than 150 feet.

The disadvantage of involving people in the loading and unloading is that this can slow down the complete system if people are not immediately available when the vehicle arrives at the workstation. The vehicles are too expensive to be used for buffer storage.

In an alternate method of transferring the load from the AGV train, the pickup and delivery station has a transfer

Figure 3.6 Demag/Barrett Model 24TEB tractor is used in an automotive plastics warehouse and manufacturing application. This driverless vehicle is shown at a loading station where this train is being loaded by a forklift truck. (Courtesy of Mannesmann Demag, Grand Rapids, Michigan)

mechanism to pull the loads off or push the loads on the trailers. For example, if a centralized storage area is used to supply the plant, the loads could be automatically transferred to the AGV trailers by a powered transfer mechanism and unloaded manually when the AGV train arrives at its proper location.

Most driverless train applications require off-line guidepath spurs, which take additional space and must be carefully planned. Usually off-line guidepath spurs are placed in receiving or shipping areas so that trains can be loaded or unloaded off the main guidepath. This feature allows a towing tractor with several trailers to pass other towing tractors with trailers that are parked at stop locations, so traffic is not obstructed.

Driverless trains come in two types of systems, closed and open. The classification depends on whether the trailers remain on the towing tractor or are uncoupled at the loading and unloading station. If the trailers remain coupled to the towing tractors, it is a closed system; if the trailers are uncoupled, it is an open system.

Automatic coupling and uncoupling of trailers is popular. Using this feature, the tractor drives into an off-line guidepath spur where it couples the trailers to the train. Upon arrival at the delivery station, the vehicle automatically uncouples the appropriate trailers. These open systems can greatly increase the efficiency of the material handling system, eliminating the operator time required to couple and uncouple the trailers.

Pallet Vehicles

Wire-guided pallet vehicles are standard walkie vehicles equipped with an electronic guidance system, commonly referred to as "stop and drop" vehicles. ("Stop and Drop" is a trademark used by Mannesmann Demag.) These vehicles were first introduced in the early 1970s and are classified as low-lift transporters.

Wire-guided pallet vehicles work best where the load movement is between two points, several hundred feet apart; load movement is from one floor position to another floor position; there is low overall material movement and a moderate number of pickup and delivery locations; and

Figure 3.7 Demag/Barrett AGV Stop and Drop™ is designed for floor-to-floor transport of pallet loads. The vehicle is available in optional single or double unit load models. For double unit load models the fork is made longer to carry two pallet loads. (Courtesy of Mannesmann Demag, Grand Rapids, Michigan)

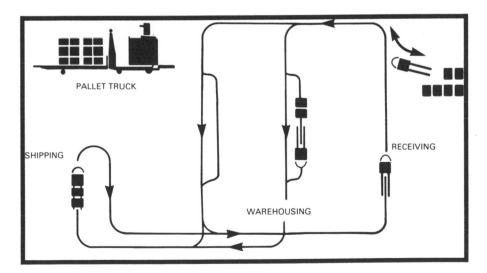

Figure 3.8 Guidepath layout for a pallet truck application. (Courtesy of Gary Koff, Mannesmann Demag, Grand Rapids, Michigan)

people are available to assist and guide the vehicle in picking up a pallet.

These vehicles have limited intelligence on board to control vehicle motions. Motions are limited to simple pickup, delivery, automatic unload, and return to the home base for the vehicle's next assignment. The typical vehicle performs a simple pickup and delivery with operator assistance in loading and unloading and operator dispatching the vehicle to the next station.

Wire-guided pallet trucks require that the loads be staged on the floor or from low shelving in pickup areas where operators can easily back the vehicle into the loads. Drop-off locations should be on off-line guidepath spurs

Figure 3.9 Hyster Movematic Pallet Carrier is designed for floor-to-floor transport of pallet loads. Photo shows both a single and a double unit load model. (Courtesy of Hyster Company, Portland, Oregon)

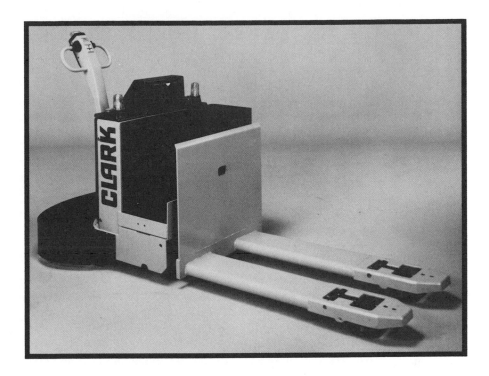

Figure 3.10 Clark AGP Series electric walkie/AutoGuide pallet truck is designed for floor-to-floor transport of pallet loads. The pallet truck is available in optional single or double unit load models. (Courtesy of Clark Material Handling Company, Lexington, Kentucky)

where the automatically delivered loads will not interfere with the traffic flow on the main guidepath.

In a typical operation the vehicle proceeds down the path to a destination requiring service, pulls onto an off-line guidepath spur, and stops. The operator working in that area boards the vehicle and guides it with a tiller steering device or a pendent control, backing the vehicle into the pallets. Manually loading the vehicle lets operators position loads anywhere off the guidepath and still be able to retrieve them. After the pallets are loaded on the vehicle, the operator dispatches it to the desired destination.

The vehicle proceeds without the operator down the main guidepath. Upon arrival at the destination, the vehicle lowers its forks, sets the load on the floor, and stops. An operator unloads the vehicle and pulls straight ahead so the forks clear the pallet. The operator then positions it back on the guidepath and dispatches the vehicle to its next destination. With automatic unload, the vehicle may automatically return empty to a loading area or home position.

The disadvantage of involving people is that it can slow down the system if people are not immediately available when the vehicle arrives at the workstation. The vehicle must not be used for buffer storage for products it is carrying.

One of the disadvantages of pallet vehicles is that their forks can snag on a lightly loaded pallet and drag or push it when depositing or picking up the pallet. This problem results from traditional American pallet construction, which features a top and bottom board. The pallet fork must fit into the pallet opening between the two boards. European pallets don't have bottom boards and as a result don't encounter this problem.

Wire-guided pallet trucks are suitable for use in installations where layouts must be easily altered or floors must be free from permanently mounted equipment. Modular designs permit some vehicles to be easily adapted to different size and shape loads. Models capable of carrying one or two pallets are available. Wire-guided pallet trucks range in load capacities from 4000 to 6500 pounds.

Aisle space requirements for guided pallet trucks are easily determined. The space required depends on the length of the vehicle, which determines its turning radius. Most guided pallet trucks are a double-pallet type and require at least twice their length to straighten out after a turn.

Unit Load Vehicles

Unit load vehicles are currently in the greatest demand and are the most standard in the industry. Each vendor has his own standard vehicle with an array of optional features; therefore, vehicle functions must be carefully evaluated because of the wide variance offered by different manufacturers.

The unit load is a highly adaptable vehicle used for many applications. Standard unit load vehicles are designed for heavy industrial use and found in all types of distribution and manufacturing industries where travel movement is

Figure 3.11 This Raymond Model 56 Electote has a chain transfer deck. The reflectors shown in the picture work with a photo sensor for the vehicle's on-board controller to determine when the loads are securely on the vehicle and have cleared the deck, indicating the vehicle is free to travel. (Courtesy of Raymond Corporation, Greene, New York)

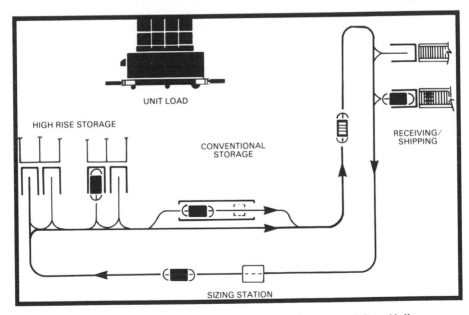

Figure 3.12 Guidepath layout for a unit load application. (Courtesy of Gary Koff, Mannesmann Demag, Grand Rapids, Michigan)

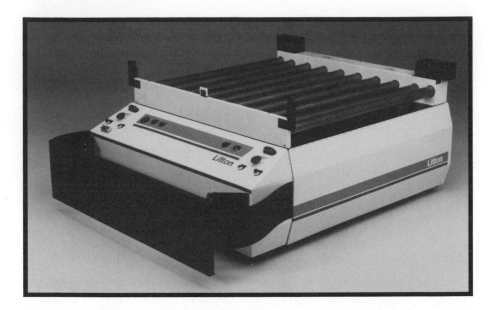

Figure 3.13 Unit Load Integrator™ vehicle from Litton has a capacity of 4000 pounds. The vehicle is fitted with a roller transfer device for interfacing with conventional conveyor systems at pickup and drop-off stations. (Courtesy of Litton Industrial Automation, Hebron, Kentucky)

high and distances are short. The most popular application for unit load vehicles is interfacing with a load stand, which can be an accumulation conveyor, the pickup and delivery station of an automatic storage and retrieval system, a single position conveyor, or a simple four-post stand.

Unit load vehicles are also quite popular in applications linking islands of automation into a totally integrated system, conveyors with storage retrieval systems, and flexible manufacturing applications.

AGV unit load applications usually involve specific assignments for individual pallet movement. These vehicles traveling over moderate distances can move high volumes of material, allowing good system versatility for product movement. These vehicles usually operate independently; with the correct guidepath layout, vehicles can take alternate routes to get to any destination. Unit load vehicles normally travel at 175 to 250 feet per minute.

These vehicles do not require much floor space and can maneuver in tight areas where other types of vehicles would be too awkward to use. While minimum guidepath turning radius for automated guided vehicles varies with the size of the vehicle, a rough guideline is 3 to 5 foot turning radius for a small unit load vehicle.

The standard unit load vehicle is designed for a specific load range and speed. Its greatest advantage is the variety of load bed configurations for standard or special applications. Standard vehicles handle single pallets, with other models designed to handle two pallets or more at a time. Load beds available include power conveyors, non-powered conveyors, dual powered conveyors, ball bearing decks, lifts for removal and pickup of loads, and special tooling for the proper nesting of loads. All these options are designed for easy automatic transfer of loads to and from fixed load

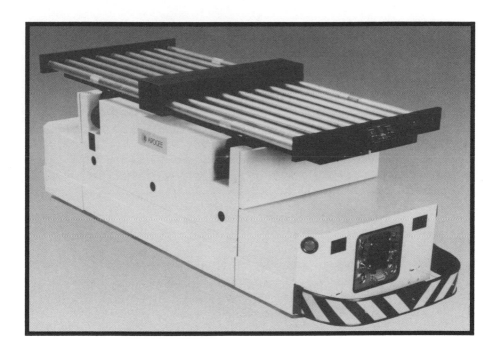

Figure 3.14 Unit load vehicle fitted with two separate conveyors using extractor wheels to power 64 workstations. Vehicle is used in a composite factory making helicopter parts. (Courtesy of Apogee Robotics, Fort Collins, Colorado)

Figure 3.15 This FMC Model UL-40 pallet vehicle handles loads up to 4000 pounds. (Courtesy of FMC Corporation, Material Handling Systems Division, Chalfont, Pennsylvania)

stands. Further description of the most common load beds follows.

Power Conveyor Roller or chain conveyor is powered by motors on the vehicle. This load bed requires the vehicle batteries to supply the power that drives the conveyor for load transfer.

Non-Powered Conveyor This load bed requires the power to be provided by the P&D station, reducing the power needed for the vehicles' batteries. The P&D stand and the vehicle are coupled together, and the loads are transferred.

Figure 3.16 Tote Integrator™ has a bi-directional shuttle transfer device to pick up and drop off totes at P&D stands. (Courtesy of Litton Industrial Automation, Hebron, Kentucky)

Shuttle Mechanism This method of load transfer is commonly referred to as a powered push/pull transfer. The shuttle mechanism can be mounted on the vehicle or on the P&D station, and used to push the load off or on the vehicle or the P&D station. With this type of device the vehicle can have a non-powered conveyor, ball bearing deck, or slides, thus reducing the battery capacity and requiring a simpler type of vehicle.

Lifts Lifts generally use electric ball screw drives for lifting and lowering the load during transfer from the vehicle to P&D station and vice versa. A mechanical torque limiter protects the lift mechanism and the motor if the lift becomes bound-up or the travel limits are exceeded.

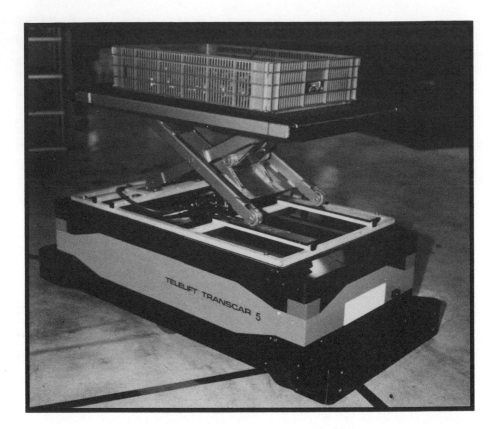

Figure 3.17 TransLogic's Integral Transcar is permanently fitted with a scissors lift for automatic loading and unloading sequences. (Courtesy of TransLogic Corporation, Denver, Colorado)

In the load stand application, the vehicle passes under the stand, stops and lifts the load so it clears the stand, drives away, and sets the load on its deck. This is a fast and efficient way to handle pallets. It should be noted that not all pallet vehicles have this capability; some do not have a single elevation deck and must pass alongside the P&D stand, or maneuver so part of the vehicle is under the P&D stand, requiring more time for proper alignment.

The disadvantage of the unit load vehicle is that all pickups and deliveries must be at the same elevation. It is also difficult to work on because it is small and compact; components are difficult to reach for adjustment and repair.

Figure 3.18 Demag/Barrett Model AGV-240C, bi-directional unit load vehicle, equipped with a powered lift/lower deck, used for picking up and handling office furniture products. (Courtesy of Mannesmann Demag, Grand Rapids, Michigan)

This can be overcome by panels and drawers that offer easy access to difficult-to-reach places.

These vehicles offer a wide range of controls. Many require an operator to manually enter the destination point and return (Category 1 control system). Other vehicles require an operator setting the return destination. More sophisticated unit load systems use computer controls, providing automatic pickup and delivery and remote management of system vehicles (Category 2 & 3).

Forklift Vehicles

AGVs are following the historical path of lift trucks and they resemble a conventional forklift truck. These vehicles have a mast and fork assembly and are used in handling pallets. The primary function of fork vehicles is to efficiently move materials moderate distances, positioning loads at different elevations. AGVs will not operate as fast as manually operated lift trucks, but they are gaining acceptance and are cost-justified in many applications.

Forklift AGVs offer several styles, including conventional, straddle, high lift, and side loading vehicles. The common denominator between these vehicles is that they are designed to transport palletized loads and position those loads at different elevations. This feature permits the vehicle to interface with many different types of equipment (conveyors, load stands, and multiple-level racks), eliminating the need for fixed-height load stands. They handle up to 4000-pound loads and can stack pallets up to 20 feet high. These vehicles require more hardware and onboard controls, and are among the most expensive vehicles. Forklift AGVs are used commonly in Category 2 and 3 control systems; thus automated fork vehicles have greater capabilities than most automated guided vehicles.

Applications of the automated fork vehicles are unlimited. In the flexible factory they can provide effective vertical buffer storage of work-in-process and stockroom material. These vehicles stack loads in racks, so the system can store work-in-process at remote buffer locations, saving floor space. They can handle a greater variety of load types including pallets, skids, and pans. Another application for forked vehicles permits assembly fixtures to be handled and moved from assembly workstation to assembly workstation until the product has been completely assembled.

The vehicle's mast can be fixed or telescopic. Fixed masts are generally used for heights up to eight feet. Beyond an eight-foot lift, a telescopic mast is recommended so the vehicle can pass through doorways and low ceiling areas. The lift mechanism is an electrical or hydraulic-driven ball screw with the fork assembly attached.

Available as optional equipment, dual forks can be fitted to the lift mechanism. This feature enables two loads to be handled at the same time, increasing the efficiency of the

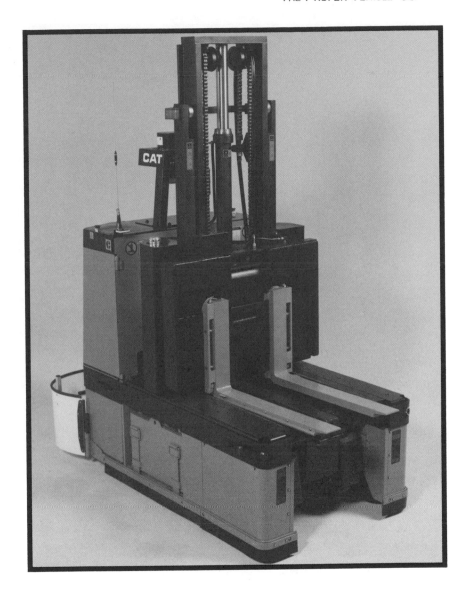

Figure 3.19 Caterpillar's Self-Guided Forklift Vehicle, Model SGL, has 4000-pound capacity, can lift loads from ground level to 96 inches, and can travel at 195 feet per minute. Fork assembly extends forward and then can be raised or lowered to the correct elevation. This feature enables the load to be contained within the vehicle while traveling. Free-ranging vehicle uses low power laser scanning of bar code targets combined with advanced dead reckoning techniques to navigate. No buried wires or stripes on the floor are needed. (Courtesy of Caterpillar Industrial, Mentor, Ohio)

Figure 3.20 This Apogee low lift straddle-type fork vehicle is used to carry out various transportation and inventory tasks among three warehouses. This vehicle can lift pallets from the floor to a maximum height of 30 inches. (Courtesy of Apogee Robotics, Fort Collins, Colorado)

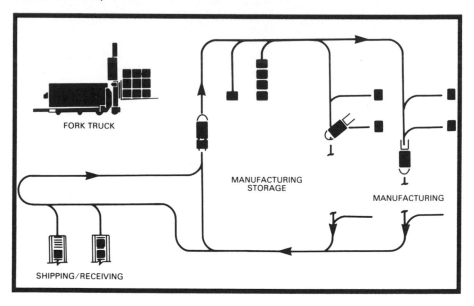

Figure 3.21 Guidepath layout for a fork type vehicle application. (Courtesy of Gary Koff, Mannesmann Demag, Grand Rapids, Michigan)

vehicle. Another option is carton clamps, which replace the fork's mechanism and are used to handle large cartons.

These vehicles travel forward with their fork pointing backwards. They are equipped with load detection devices and bumpers for traveling forward; for traveling in reverse, the load detection devices are limited. Photo eyes in the body of the vehicle, the tips of the forks, and the outriggers detect objects in the way of the vehicle, find the load center, and enter the pallet openings without disturbing the load. If the vehicle hits an obstruction in entering a pickup station, it shuts down.

When traveling in reverse, the vehicle operates at a reduced speed. The vehicle usually travels in reverse only when it is approaching the load to be picked up or in the final positioning of a load to be deposited. As the vehicle approaches the P&D stand, it stops, positions the forks for

Figure 3.22 This FMC Model FV-40/80 fork type vehicle has a clamp attachment for handling bales of fiber. The clamp secures the load, and the friction between the clamp surface and the material holds the load. Also note the vehicle has a foam bumper. Vehicle capacity is 3000 pounds. (Courtesy of FMC Corporation, Material Handling Systems Division, Chalfont, Pennsylvania)

the pickup, and approaches the load stand, where the forks are inserted in the pallet opening. The loaded forks are positioned close to the floor when the vehicle is traveling to insure safety and stability of the load and vehicle.

In addition, when the load is in an elevated position on the vehicle, the travel speed is restricted. This is to eliminate any stability problems with the load or vehicle. When the load is in the lowest position, the travel position, the vehicle speed is not restricted.

One of the disadvantages of this type of vehicle is that product handling is relatively slow, because the extra vehicle movements require more time (i.e. to lift the loads and position the vehicle for load pickup). In some cases the time required for stacking or rack storage applications cannot be justified because of low throughput.

Another disadvantage is that these vehicles require wider aisles for backing into pickup and delivery points. Aisle space can be reduced by adding dual drives on the vehicle to improve its maneuverability. This feature is commonly found on large fork vehicles. In addition, these vehicles are higher priced than other vehicles.

Conventional or Counterbalanced Vehicles This vehicle has the outrigger (straddle arms) beneath the fork. In the fork's lowest position, the arms are on top of the outriggers. (Some manufacturers have developed a term "inrigger" or "fork on top of rigger.") They cannot pick up standard pallets directly from the floor because of the outrigger's position; it prevents the forks from being lowered to floor level—its lowest position is a couple of inches off the ground. This configuration offers an advantage: because the outriggers are beneath the forks, the width requirement of a vehicle is cut 16 to 20 inches, omitting the space required for the outriggers. In addition the length of the vehicle is stretched, providing a more stable vehicle. Because of the narrower and longer profile, the pivot radius and maneuverability change in comparison to the straddle-type vehicle.

Straddle-Type Vehicles Straddle fork vehicles have straddle arms or outriggers outside the fork to help stabilize the vehicle. This enables the forks to be positioned on the floor so standard pallets can be picked up off the floor. If the outriggers are directly under the forks, the forks cannot be

Figure 3.23 Roberts' TrakStar Model RTA-40EF12 is equipped with an electro-mechanical ball screw lift. The position of the forks over the support legs limits the type of pallets to be picked up from the floor. (Courtesy of Roberts Corporation, Lansing, Michigan)

positioned on the floor and therefore cannot be positioned beneath a pallet. These vehicles are designed to lift loads from floor level to different elevations. The limitation with straddle vehicles is that their outriggers may interfere with the loads adjacent to the load being picked up, preventing loads from being positioned side-by-side.

High Lift Vehicles The high lift vehicle is a relatively new straddle-type fork vehicle, developed as users have wanted loads lifted higher and higher. They can automatically pick up and deposit loads on the floor and at elevated heights, up to 20 feet, without human interface.

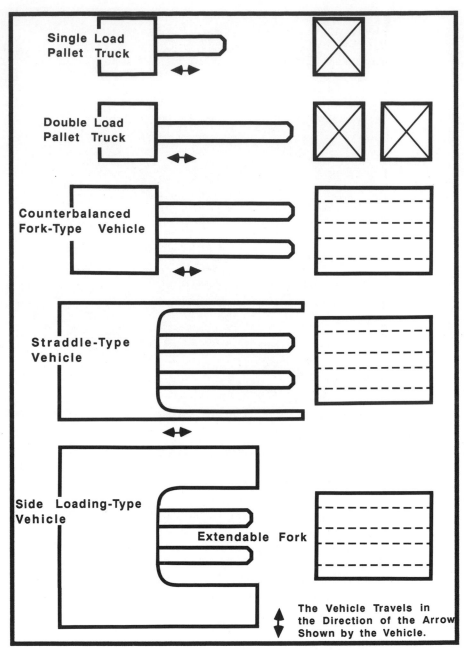

Figure 3.24 Plan view of the family of fork-type vehicle. Single load pallet vehicle, double load pallet vehicle, counterbalanced fork-type vehicle, straddle-type vehicle, and side loading-type vehicle.

Side Loading Vehicles This vehicle consists of the fork assembly mounted on a turret, which allows the forks to be extended sideways from the vehicle. One type of side loading vehicle can pick up loads from the floor, enter an aisle, swing the load to either side and deposit it in a rack.

Figure 3.25 This FMC Model FV-40HL high lift fork-type vehicle is a straddle vehicle. It can lift 4000-pound loads from ground level to an elevation of 15 feet. (Courtesy of FMC Corporation, Material Handling Systems Division, Chalfont, Pennsylvania)

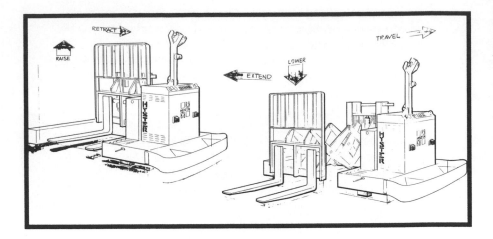

Figure 3.26 Hyster side loading vehicle adds versatility to fork-type vehicle by providing side loading capability, fork reach, and fork lift. (Courtesy of Hyster Company, Portland, Oregon)

Another type of side loading vehicle has the forks permanently mounted perpendicular to the direction of travel. These vehicles do not rotate about the mast; rather, the mast extends in and out perpendicular to the direction of travel. With the second type of vehicle the position of the load to be picked up must be coordinated with the position of the vehicle with respect to the aisle. The advantage of side loading vehicles is that they require less aisle space and reduced cycle time because special maneuvering of the vehicle is eliminated. These vehicles are the most expensive type of fork vehicles.

Light Load Vehicles and Module Transport Vehicles

Light load vehicles have been developed as a result of the success AGVs have had in other applications. Small, lightweight, low-cost, computer-controlled vehicles are needed to bring greater flexibility to small parts handling. This type of vehicle is a unit load vehicle with a lighter payload. Light load vehicles have capacities of approximately 500 pounds or less and are used to transport small parts, baskets, trays, or other light loads through hospitals, offices, and light manufacturing environments. They are designed to operate in areas with limited space.

Module transport vehicles are frequently used as a towing vehicle to transport one trolley or cart throughout a facility. The vehicle drives underneath the trolley and automatically couples to the trolley, takes the trolley to its destination and uncouples it, and proceeds to the next assignment. The trolleys have swivel casters made from hard rubber to support the trolley frame. Trolleys are designed to transport mail, meals, material waste, and industrial containers. These vehicles are being used for many industrial and commercial applications.

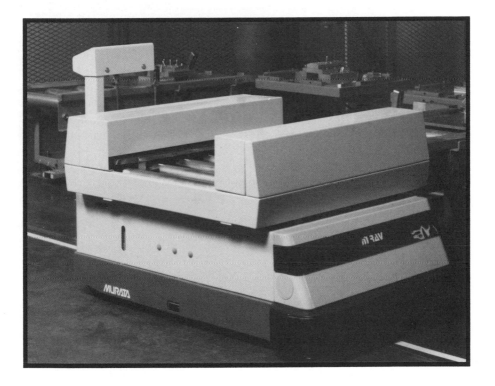

Figure 3.27 Tape Guided Murata Model RAV1 AGV with roller conveyor has a capacity of 220 pounds and is used for transporting light loads. The vehicle is a uni-directional vehicle that is optically guided. (Courtesy of Murata of America, Troy, Michigan)

Figure 3.28 This vehicle, fitted with shelving for carrying light loads, is part of a system that moves raw materials and work-in-process items through an electronics manufacturer's plant. The system's 2400 feet of guidepath run over a variety of surfaces, including tile, concrete, and carpeting. This system performs 50-80% of the materials handling trips formerly made by the previous manual material handling system. Note the retroreflective tape on the floor, which the vehicle uses as its guidepath. (Courtesy of Apogee Robotics, Fort Collins, Colorado)

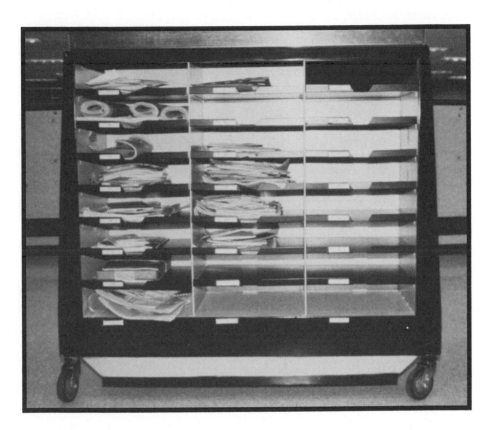

Figure 3.29 Many different trolleys can be transported by TransLogic's Interchangeable Transcar such as this open mail bin trolley. Since trolleys are detachable, they can be loaded and unloaded while the vehicle is making deliveries with another trolley. (Courtesy of TransLogic Corporation, Denver, Colorado)

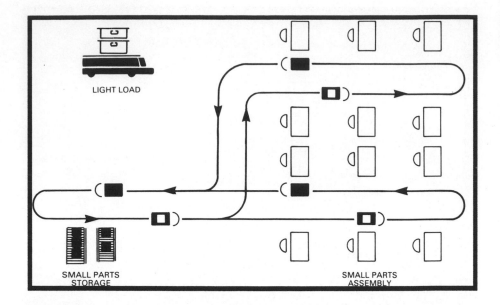

Figure 3.30 Guidepath layout for a light load vehicle application. (Courtesy of Gary Koff, Mannesmann Demag, Grand Rapids, Michigan)

Figure 3.31 Dietary trolleys are loaded with meal trays for transport to hospital wards for three meals per day. TransLogic's Interchangeable Transcar also transports laundry, trash, and supplies throughout multi-floor facilities by following a passive stainless steel guide tape. Dietary and laundry trolleys are sanitized by a cart wash upon their return. (Courtesy of TransLogic Corporation, Denver, Colorado)

Figure 3.32 Control Engineering Company Medicar vehicle used to transport a cart to deliver material throughout a hospital. The load is transported by being carried on the deck of the vehicle. The cart has its own wheels so it can be easily guided when it is not being transported by the vehicle. (Courtesy of Control Engineering Company, Harbor Springs, Michigan)

Figure 3.33 Apogee vehicle, with carts, used both inside and outside to transport food, laundry, and trash in the Santa Rita jail. The vehicle lifts the cart off the ground to transport the cart. The smooth, stainless steel vehicle shells forestall tampering or smuggling of contraband. The vehicles use fiber nickel cadmium batteries, charged through opportunity floor contacts with a quick recharge feature. (Courtesy of Apogee Robotics, Fort Collins, Colorado)

Figure 3.34 This vehicle is used to transport laundry in a hospital. Trolleys designed for transporting laundry are towed by TransLogic's Interchangeable Transcar across a scale for weighing. Scale surface is free of metal for 1" depth to allow operation with the passive stainless steel guide tape. Meals, trash, and supplies are also transported by Transcar throughout multi-floor hospitals by using different trolleys. (Courtesy of TransLogic Corporation, Denver, Colorado)

Typical applications include:

- Hospital use, where the vehicles deliver linens, surgical supplies, and food throughout the entire hospital.

- Office use, where vehicles deliver mail throughout offices, using a guidewire installed under the carpeting.

- Light assembly use, where vehicles distribute small parts from a storage area to individual workstations.

- Parts kitting applications, where the vehicles deliver different parts to be assembled into kits.

Special Vehicles

Any of the above standard vehicles can be customized for a special application and be considered a special vehicle. The possibilities are unlimited. Vehicles can be designed for particular environments (cold rooms, clean rooms, hazardous areas), heavy payloads, special handling requirements, special vehicle platforms, and assembly system applications. The disadvantages of the special vehicle are the high engineering and manufacturing costs, and the unproven performance of the vehicle prior to installation.

The assembly type of vehicle fits the general classifications of a special vehicle. These vehicles are designed for a specific product to be carried and assembled on. They require product positioning lifts, other equipment to interface with the assembly people and robots, and product transferring equipment. Vehicles have been designed to handle full-size automobiles, trucks, and construction equipment.

The average AGV capacity is between 2000 to 6000 pounds; however, there is no limit to the practical capacity of an AGV. Heavy payload AGVs with capacity of 100,000 pounds are used to move dies, coiled steel, and sheet steel through warehousing operations and production processes, and in the paper industry to move large rolls of paper from the mills. These heavy loads were previously handled and transported by using overhead cranes.

While the special vehicles are high capacity, they still have many of the attributes commonly found in other vehicles. High capacity special vehicles have speeds up to 250 feet per minute in automatic mode of operation, tight turning radius relative to the vehicle size, battery power (although some vehicles can be powered by internal combustion engines), and small vehicle profiles in relationship to the load size.

Specialized vehicles are being developed for other industries to handle unusual shaped products or for automatic delivery and loading of supplies or tools needed on a manufacturing line.

Figure 3.35 This vehicle has a 70,000 pound capacity and transports mix bowls in the manufacture of solid rocket fuel. It is powered by an 85-horsepower diesel engine. (Courtesy of Mentor AGVS, Inc., Mentor, Ohio)

Another special application for AGVs features a robot mounted on the vehicle platform to perform loading and unloading operations. These mobile robots can travel to fixed assembly stations and perform an assembly task. This enables the robot to be better utilized in more applications.

Figure 3.36 This vehicle is designed to assemble off-road heavy earth moving equipment with load capacity of 95,000 pounds, load length of 13'4" to 37' 7". The vehicle is 20" high, with a wheelbase of 252", and a maximum travelling speed of 200 FPM. The system has 25,000 feet of guidepath, over 25 miles of in-floor wiring, and serves 77 drop spurs. (Courtesy of Elwell-Parker, Cleveland, Ohio and Control Engineering, Harbor Springs, Michigan)

Figure 3.37 The vehicle shown is a Raymond Model 57 used for a special application. The AGV has a fifth wheel for trailer hook-up. The vehicle pulls a trailer that is loaded by an 8000-pound locomotive engine. (Courtesy of Raymond Corporation, Greene, New York)

Figure 3.38 This AGV moves 60,000 pound aluminum coils through the entire mill process. The coil length is 80" and diameter ranges from 96" to 48". The system has 8000 feet of guidepath serving 33 P&D stations. (Courtesy of Elwell-Parker, Cleveland, Ohio and Control Engineering, Harbor Springs, Michigan)

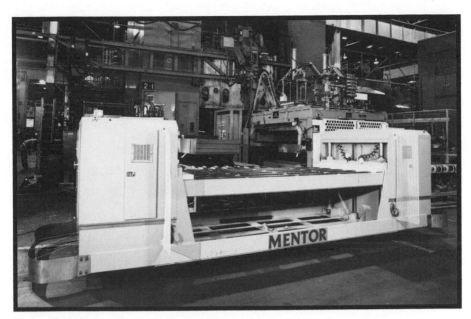

Figure 3.39 This vehicle has a 15,000 pound capacity and is designed for moving sheet metal blanks from the blanker to the head of the press line at U. S. automaker's stamping plant. (Courtesy of Mentor AGVS, Inc., Mentor, Ohio)

Figure 3.40 Automated guided vehicle system with a customized control system delivers and picks up sub-assemblies from work islands. Vehicles serve as assembly platforms, and as destination-controlled workpiece transport. Vehicle guidance is accomplished inductively via central stationary controls or coordinate mapping with an on-board microprocessor. (Courtesy of Eisenmann Corporation, Crystal Lake, Illinois)

Summary Comparison

Table 3.1 provides a quick summary of the different type vehicles discussed. The capacity, lift, relative cost range, and speed are outlined.

TABLE 3.1 VEHICLE COMPARISON

TYPE VEHICLE	STANDARD CAPACITY K LBS	LIFT	ESTIMATED COST	FPM
DRIVERLESS TRAINS	2-50	0"	$35K-50K	100-400
PALLET VEHICLE	4-6.5	8"-12"	$25K-40K	50-250
STANDARD UNIT LOAD	1-8	12"	$35K-65K	100-250
FORK VEHICLE	4-20	49"-240"	$60K-90K	150-250
LIGHTWEIGHT VEHICLES	.1-1	0"	$25K-50K	50-100
SPECIAL VEHICLES	15-100	NOT RESTRICTED	$75K-250K	80-250

FUTURE AGV REQUIREMENTS

This chapter on the proper vehicle would not be complete without a discussion on what the future vehicle requirements will most likely be. The following list of ideas suggests standard vehicle attributes of the future:

- A zero turning radius, providing the highest degree of maneuverability. This will become a standard feature rather than a special option.

- A narrower profile vehicle. Since the floor space between machines is at a premium, it makes sense that the AGV pathways be as narrow as possible. This requires a more maneuverable vehicle with better sensory capabilities and a smarter host computer.

- A more intelligent on-board controller with improved diagnostics.

- A more intelligent host computer system with improved diagnostics.

- On-board and off-board software that is friendlier and that makes path changes easier.

- Personal computers that control 50- to 60-vehicle systems.

- Higher communication rates for radio communications, enabling them to be used for larger AGV systems.

- Enhanced vehicle communications and interfacing with the host computer and with other equipment in the plant.

- Enhanced sensory capabilities for navigation and collision avoidance. Advanced technology with inertial guidance, machine vision, and lasers will become an important part of future AGVs. These technologies will give AGV systems more flexibility and improved navigation systems providing trackless control.

- More standard and less costly vehicles that are more reliable and flexible.

- Payloads less than 50 pounds.

- Rough terrain vehicles.

- Faster vehicles. As the reliability of the AGV safety system improves, the vehicle speed will increase, and fewer vehicles will be required for the system.

- AGVs carrying robots to provide a mobile robot system, traveling to various fixed assembly stations to perform specific tasks. These tasks may be required to reduce contamination and restrict human contact with the product and process.

- Full 3-shift operation without battery recharging.

- Fiber nickel cadmium batteries will be used to provide fast charging and long life while increasing the utilization of the vehicles.

Figure 4.1 Gull-wing feature on Unit Load Integrator™ vehicle shows panel lift open
for easy access to service vehicle electronics and drive. This photo displays the
front drive wheel with the tracking optical head, idle wheel, and electric fuse board.
(Courtesy of Litton Industrial Automation, Hebron, Kentucky)

4 AGV FEATURES AND FLOOR CONSIDERATIONS

Because so many features can be incorporated in a vehicle, it is important that a chapter of this book be devoted to the features that make up the vehicle design and the floor with which the vehicle must interface.

In a totally automated factory, the vehicles may operate up to 168 hours per week, the equivalent of four 40-hour shifts. The typical United States factory does not operate at its full capacity. However, automation equipment typically runs 30% to 80% more than in a conventional plant. Thus, when considering automation, plan on using the equipment at least twice as much as conventional machines. Make sure the vehicle designs are simple, with as few moving parts as possible, requiring a minimum number of adjustments. The vehicles must be reliable and easy to maintain. The importance of this cannot be underestimated.

This chapter discusses the following subjects:

Mode of Operation	AGV Envelope
Console Panels	Vehicle Articulation
Drive Wheels	Guidance Systems
Measuring Wheels	Floor Ramps
Antennas	Doors/Elevators
Steering Control	Floor Design
Drive-Steering Geometries	Pallets
Vehicle Positioning	

MODE OF OPERATION

AGVs have three modes of operation: automatic, semiautomatic, and manual. The automatic mode offers all three categories of control, providing all system functions (on-board and off-board) and equipment movements. The semiautomatic mode allows the equipment to be controlled by manually keying in commands. This is typically used for troubleshooting a vehicle, or for sending a vehicle to an area for maintenance.

Manual mode is provided by a pendent controller. Pendent controllers can be either built in or plugged into the vehicle; plug-in controllers prevent unauthorized use of the vehicle. The pendent controller enables the vehicle to be steered, the load bed operated, and the vehicle controlled at variable speed. When the vehicle is operated in manual mode, there is no communication between the vehicle and the computer control system.

Manual operation of AGV equipment is important for emergency use of the vehicle. If a vehicle malfunctions and cannot be moved under automatic control, or there is a power outage and a vehicle has to be moved, the vehicle can be removed from the system manually.

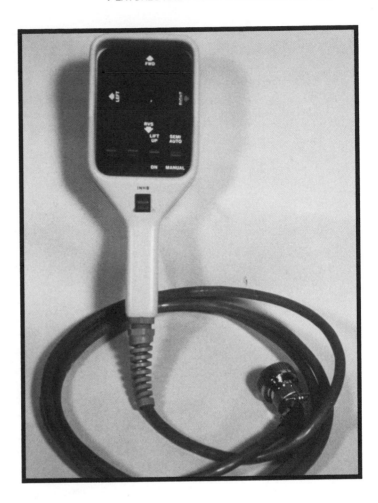

Figure 4.2 This photo shows a pendent control that can be removed from the vehicle. It is used to control a disabled vehicle and remove it from the guidepath. The pendent also controls load handling features on the vehicle such as lift (up/down), roller deck (right/left), etc. (Courtesy of FMC Corporation, Material Handling Systems Division, Chalfont, Pennsylvania)

Pallet vehicles and towing vehicles have the operator controls permanently mounted on the vehicle. Thus, when a vehicle requires an operator interface, the operator has easy access to the controls. The operator manually boards the vehicle and positions it for a pallet pickup or at a P&D stand.

CONSOLE PANELS

All vehicles have console panels but they will vary in complexity depending on the type vehicle used. The console panel will typically have an alphanumeric keyboard, digital readout, key switch, and indicator lights. Console panels have the following functions:

- The entry panel's alphanumeric keyboard and digital readout display allow for manual address programming of the vehicle. In Category 1 systems this is the method used to dispatch the vehicle. In

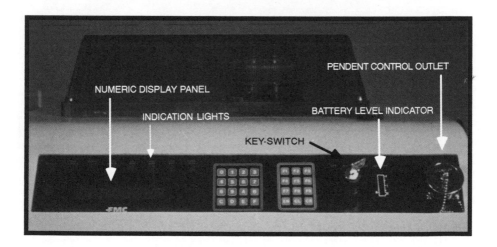

Figure 4.3 This picture shows the on-board vehicle control panel. Operator indication lights include: vehicle on wire, vehicle in manual mode of operation, emergency stop condition, low battery, battery charge if opportunity charging, and software errors. An L.E.D. panel provides diagnostic information. The panel also has a numeric display panel, a key-switch for controlling the off/on status on the vehicle, a battery level indicator, and the outlet for the pendent control. (Courtesy of FMC Corporation, Material Handling Systems Division, Chalfont, Pennsylvania)

more complex systems, the entry panel lets operators program and dispatch a vehicle when the control system is not operating.

- The digital display allows for visual verification of data input, data output, guidepath frequency vehicle is traveling on, and next destination address. It is also used to read error messages for troubleshooting vehicle functions.

- The key switch is to limit vehicle operation to authorized personnel only, and to select the mode of operation: manual, automatic, or out of service.

- Indicator lights are prominently displayed on each vehicle and communicate vehicle status. The number of indicator lights depends on the type of vehicle used, the type of system (Category 1, 2, or 3), and if the vehicle is standard or a custom design. Typical vehicle status lights indicate:

  - Vehicle is operational/Controller is ready
  - Vehicle off the guidepath
  - Vehicle blocked
  - Vehicle loaded
  - Manual mode of operation
  - Automatic mode of operation
  - Battery needs charging
  - Emergency stop
  - Software error
  - Lift is up
  - Lift is down

DRIVE WHEELS

If the drive wheels fail or lock up and the vehicle cannot be driven with the pendent control, the vehicle must be moved another way. Typically, the vehicle will have spring-loaded drive wheels that can be jacked off the ground, with an idle wheel jack assembly, so the AGV can be pushed out of the way.

Spring-loaded drive wheels also put constant pressure on the floor, keeping wheels from spinning on uneven ground. The drive wheel can be released from floor contact and the AGV easily pushed.

All drive wheels should be designed to give the vehicle the capability of climbing a 10% slope at rated capacity.

While most vehicles use direct current stored in batteries to power the vehicle, some use internal combustion engines.

MEASURING WHEELS

A measuring wheel is used 1) to enable the vehicle to travel off the guidepath (off-wire guidance is also called "dead reckoning"); 2) to assist in navigation of the vehicle, determining its relative location on the guidepath; and 3) to improve the vehicle's positioning accuracy.

In dead reckoning, as the vehicle is ready to leave the wire, the measuring wheel is zeroed, the vehicle's steering is locked, and the vehicle begins traveling. As the vehicle travels, the microprocessor counts the encoder pulses and computes the number of wheel rotations traveled off the guidepath. When the vehicle is ready to return to the wire, it reverses the process. Vehicles can dead reckon a turn (U-turns used to turn to a parallel path and travel in a different direction, right angle turns at intersection), radius turns of two to ten feet, rotating the vehicle about its center, straight lines (over manhole covers and railroad crossings), or other maneuvers, and then reenter the guidepath at the original point or at another guidepath location.

The distance the vehicle can travel off the guidepath is limited because the only known reference is the starting point. After the vehicle travels 10 to 30 feet, the accumulation of error due to wheel slippage, bumpiness in uneven floors, and electrical interference can become too great for the vehicle to successfully return to the guidepath. With short traveling distances, dead reckoning can be accurate enough for positioning to a P&D station.

The benefit of the off-wire guidance is that it can operate a vehicle where it would be difficult to run a guidewire. Some vehicles have the capability to "dead reckon" during normal guidepath travel and in making turns. This feature enables vehicles to cross steel plates located in the floor.

While it has been proved that dead reckoning can function, in actual practice it is reliable only in the simplest applications. It is suggested that this technique be used only if there are no more reliable alternatives.

The measuring wheel has optical incremental encoders which are connected to each idle wheel on both sides of the vehicle. It is important that the measuring wheel be an idle wheel and not a drive wheel. This is to prevent slippage, which will occur with a driven wheel. If the encoder wheel slips, the on-board microprocessor records the vehicle as traveling a given distance, when actually it was recording the wheel spinning. When the encoders are connected to the idle wheels, they are not affected by drive wheel slippage.

The measuring wheel measures distance within 1% accuracy. These encoders can detect a circumferential movement of each drive wheel of less than 0.1mm. To make sure the 1% error doesn't cause problems, through the accumulation of errors, reference points are put in the guidepath system. These reference points are then used as "0" points for the system measuring wheel to start at. The vehicle is always looking for these references and measuring the distance between the references. A typical command might be to cross reference F and then go 12 feet and drop the load.

The idle wheels drive the encoders by rotating running shafts inside stationary supporting stub axles. As the wheels rotate they generate pulses by an encoder, which are counted and recorded by the microprocessor on-board the vehicle. Summing both the encoder counts indicates the distance traveled, while the differences between the counts will be proportional to the angle turned by the vehicle. These pulses indicate the distance the vehicle has traveled from the known reference points. This feature allows the controller to know the relative position of the vehicle at all times. In other systems the controller only knows where the vehicle is when it passes a communication point or code plates, passes from zone to zone, or passes some other point of reference.

The benefits and purpose of using the measuring wheel include:

- Helping vehicles navigate and verifying the vehicle location.

- Determining at what point a vehicle changing guidepaths should start searching for the new frequency.

- Simplifying the floor layout so the number of communication points can be reduced and programming is simpler.

- Enabling a vehicle to operate off the guidepath for short distances and return to the wire. Some vehicles can dead reckon during normal guidepath travel and in making turns. This feature enables vehicles to cross steel plates located in the floor.

Antennas

The antenna for inductive communication can be mounted to the drive/steer unit. Communication between the AGV and the controller takes place when this antenna is located over a communication loop that is embedded in the floor.

Each vehicle can have as many as six antennas, at different locations on the vehicle so they can pick up different signals from cables in the floor. One antenna is used for stopping, one or two antennas for steering, one for communication, and two for special vehicle functions. The on-board microprocessor is used in controlling the antennas.

Steering Control

All inductive guidance systems use a steering control to follow the signal in the guidepath. The steering control unit consists of two coils which make up the steering antenna. Two steering antennas are generally mounted on the drive wheel. This makes the steering of the AGV much easier to control. One steering antenna is mounted in front of the drive wheel for the forward direction and one is mounted for the reverse direction, with only one steering antenna activated at a time. This type of steering control is used on all types of AGVs.

The steering antenna is positioned over the guidewire, detecting the magnetic field in the guidewire, following the wire throughout the system. The signal is transmitted to the steering control unit, which controls the direct current steering servo-motor. The vehicle's steering control unit compares the intensity of the magnetic field in the two sensor coils, and if a discrepancy is detected the servo-motor will steer the vehicle to the right or to the left. (See Figure 4.10.)

The further the antenna is located from the drive motor, the better the steering accuracy. The AGV steers based on the angle of the antenna to the drive wheel; the greater the distance of the antenna from the center of the wheel, the smaller the angle before steering correction is made.

The steering servo-motor, the drive motor, and transmission are mounted on the wheel assembly; both motors are DC permanent magnet motors. There can be limit switches mounted on the wheel assembly for monitoring the travel speed at various steering angles: traveling in a straight line at a pre-set speed, and traveling around curves at a reduced speed. The maximum steering angle for a vehicle which travels in both the forward and reverse direction is approximately 60 to 70 degrees. The maximum steering angle for a vehicle which must travel perpendicular to the normal direction of travel must be 90 degrees.

Drive-Steering Geometries

Vehicles are available with different wheel geometries for steering and maneuvering. The type of geometry depends on the vendor's preference and the guidepath layout, aisle width, P&D or workstation alignment tolerance, and versatility of the transfer mechanism on the vehicle. There can be a number of steering and drive wheel combinations. Many of the steering geometries use a dual steering system to improve mobility of the vehicle. Dual steering can provide side travel capability at reduced speeds, although this feature is available with only a few vehicles. A dual drive system is also used to improve vehicle traction and the handling of heavily loaded vehicles.

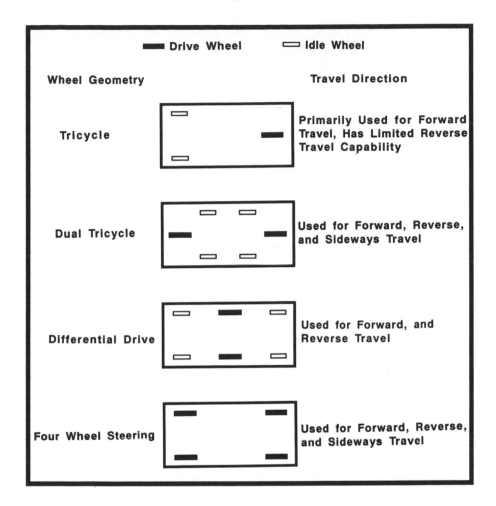

Figure 4.4 Drive-steering geometries used to drive and maneuver the vehicle.

Steering systems available from different manufacturers include:

Tricycle Wheel Geometry

This geometry consists of three wheels, with a single wheel for steering and driving the vehicle. The drive wheel is spring-loaded, located in the front of the vehicle, and pulls the vehicle on the guidepath. Tricycle vehicles with a wide wheel base do not track well, especially in reverse, because the idle wheels move away from the guidepath. When reverse travel is required, the antenna for the reverse direction must be mounted in the rear of the vehicle. Vehicle speed will be reduced to 40 feet per minute. This tracking characteristic has to be considered in the guidepath layout.

The spring-loaded drive wheel can be raised off the ground for pushing an immobilized vehicle. When the wheel is raised, two casters built in the chassis support the vehicle. When the floor condition is oily and traction is poor, the single driven wheel is likely to slip; this can sometimes be prevented by using a dual drive vehicle.

Dual Tricycle Wheel Geometry

The dual tricycle is made up of two tricycle wheel assemblies providing independent steering and drive wheels in the front and the rear of the vehicle, with caster wheels on the sides of the vehicle. This wheel geometry has the capability to travel in forward and reverse, to corner, to rotate about its central axis, and to travel sideways.

Vehicles with power-steered front and rear axles are superior to vehicles with only one power-steered axle. The dual power-steered axle wheel geometry is used when the vehicle and load are long. To improve the mobility even more, two guidepaths can be used to minimize the space and time required for long vehicles to travel through a corner or curve in the guidepath, and to straighten out the vehicle after the curve much more rapidly; this is typically used with long assembly vehicles.

The dual independent drives increase the vehicle's maneuverability and improve its capacity for traveling up ramps. As the vehicle travels up a ramp, the center of gravity load vector shifts to the trailing wheels. If the vehicle had only front-wheel drive, the reduced load on the drive wheels would reduce traction.

Differential Drive Wheel Geometry

This wheel geometry consists of two fixed, independently-driven drives mounted towards the outside of the vehicle, in the middle, with caster wheels at the corners to provide stability. The steering antenna on these vehicles rides over the guidepath, receiving the signal. The steering control balances out the signal in the steering antenna by either speeding up or slowing down one of the drive motors. The vehicle is steered by varying the speed and direction of each drive; if the drive wheels are driven in different directions at different speeds, the vehicle can rotate about its center and negotiate a turn. To move the vehicle forward or in reverse, the wheels are driven together.

The advantage of the differential drive wheel geometry is the limited space required to maneuver the vehicle. This makes the vehicle very maneuverable and reduces considerably the guidepath space required; in fact turns can be made in 90 degrees. However, it should be pointed out that a normal radius guidepath curve can handle a higher volume of traffic (higher throughput volume) than the 90-degree turn guidepath systems.

Four-Wheel Steering Geometry

The four-wheel steering geometry is used for special applications. This design combines a number of steering units and drive wheels. If all four wheels have steering capability, the vehicle can be maneuvered in turns and travel forward, in reverse, and sideways. These vehicles do not have a preferred direction of travel and can travel the same speed in both directions. This wheel geometry is also used for heavy payload applications and can be helpful in adjusting the vehicle's position at a transfer station.

Uni-Directional and Bi-Directional Vehicles

Vehicles are generally classified as either uni-directional or bi-directional. A uni-directional vehicle is one which travels predominantly in one direction. A uni-directional vehicle can have reversing capability but it is slow and awkward in traveling in the reverse direction. A bi-directional vehicle travels in both forward and reverse to accurately position loads and to return from dead-end aisles to the main guidepath simply by reversing direction. For most bi-directional vehicles, reverse speed is approximately 50% that of full forward speed, and creep speed is 10% to 20% of full speed. Some vehicles can travel in forward and reverse at equal speeds.

Vehicle Positioning

Positioning accuracy is important for the AGV, ranging from plus or minus three inches to plus or minus 0.010 inches, depending on the interface requirements. A well-designed system plus a good vehicle can typically achieve a better accuracy than plus or minus 0.25 inches without the use of positioning cones. Most AGV manufacturers claim that their vehicles can achieve a positioning accuracy of plus or minus 0.125 inches without any special equipment.

The more precise the positioning requirements, the more time required for the vehicle to dock up with stationary equipment. This can add 15 to 60 seconds at each pickup or delivery, slowing the system's throughput. Thus it is important to make sure that the position requirements are not over-specified.

Interface Method	Tolerance
Manual load and unload	plus/minus 3 in.
Conveyor interface	plus/minus 1 in.
ASRS P&D station	plus/minus 0.25 in.
Machine tool interface	plus/minus 0.010 in.

To improve positioning accuracy and repeatability of the AGV at the P&D stand, the vehicle is provided with positioning cones, which accurately hold the pallet while the vehicle travels. Positioning cones are also used on the P&D stands to accurately locate the pallet before the transfer is made between the vehicle and P&D stand. The pallet that the vehicle is carrying is lowered into the positioning cones in the floor or on the P&D stand. At the bottom of the pallet there are two pairs of sockets, one pair to locate the pallet on the vehicle and the other to locate the pallet on the P&D

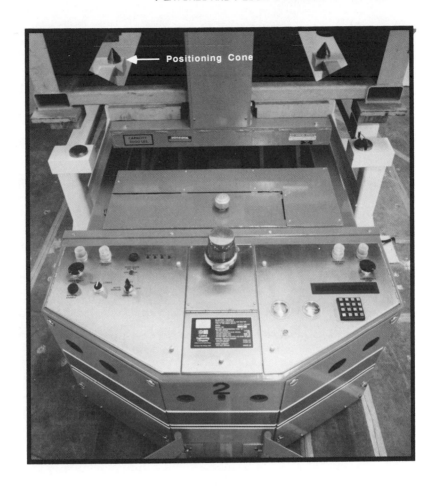

Figure 4.5 Control Engineering Company Auto-Trans vehicle is depositing a tool rack on a P&D stand. The P&D stand is equipped with positioning cones for accurate alignment of the tool rack. The positioning cones are shown in the back of the photo. (Courtesy of Control Engineering Company, Harbor Springs, Michigan)

stand. As the pallet is set down, the sockets and tapered cones slide together. These positioning cones are required for automatic transfers and for robotic applications requiring extraordinary positioning accuracy.

AGV Envelope

Normally, the physical envelope of the AGV is increased by 18 inches on all sides to assure separation between the AGV and any building columns or obstructions. Opposing guidepaths must be separated by the greatest load width plus 18 inches. This is particularly critical on turns or through doorways. There are two common exceptions to the 18 inches rule: 1) where safety considerations dictate greater space for personnel, and 2) where the physical interface with another piece of equipment requires closer spacing (e.g., P&D stands).

Vehicle Articulation

Vehicle articulation is a common feature of unit load vehicles. The vehicle frame is built with a hinge joint in the middle of the vehicle, allowing the vehicle to flex. This feature enables the vehicle to better travel on steep ramps and is especially beneficial in plants with uneven and irregular floors, because it enables the drive wheels to maintain constant contact with the floor.

Guidance Systems

As a vehicle travels throughout factory aisles, it needs a continuous reference for easy navigation. Guidance systems play an important role in every successful AGV system, yet are the component most often taken for granted.

There are four general types of AGV guidance systems: 1) Passive guidance systems, which have optical paths, chemical paths, or metal tape; 2) Three-dimensional (3-D) tracking systems, which require landmarks or code plates fixed to the building structure and factory walls wherever the vehicle needs a location reference; 3) The newest type of guidance systems, the grid method, in which the guidepath is laid out in a grid or checkerboard pattern and the vehicle navigates from the reference grid layout; 4) Inductive guidance systems, which use guidewires placed in the floor to provide a signal for the vehicle to follow. These systems are the most popular because of their reliability, and the ability to incorporate navigation reference points, stop points, and in some applications a means of communication to the vehicle. The technology for inductive guidepaths is well-established and can be obtained at a reasonable cost. This is the type of guidance used by most AGV manufacturers. (It should be pointed out that similar guidance techniques from different manufacturers are not compatible.)

Every guidance system should provide a means to guide the vehicle reliably throughout the system, avoiding collision with stationary objects, people, and other vehicles, and accurate vehicle navigation to known reference points, so the system controller knows the location of all vehicles operating within the system. Other attributes to be evaluated include the length of guidepath that can be accommodated by the technology, the accuracy with which vehicles can track the guidepath, flexibility in moving the guidepath, guidepath reliability, difficulty of installation, and equipment cost. None of the above guidance systems completely satisfies all of these requirements; compromises must be made to select the optimum system for the application.

Passive Guidepaths

Passive guidepaths are used extensively in the electronic, light assembly, and processing businesses, in office environments, and in some industrial applications. These systems are excellent for clean environments, and have the advantages of accurate tracking and extreme flexibility in changing the route or adding guidepath. Passive guidepaths are the least expensive of all guidepath systems and can be installed in a couple of days without disrupting an existing operation.

Communication to the AGV computer control cannot be incorporated in a passive guidepath. The traffic control is independent from the guidepath, and in most systems the traffic controller communicates with each vehicle using a radio or an infrared medium.

Two common passive guidepaths use optical technology. The first relies on reflective contrast recognition of the guidepath, and the second method is based on stimulated emission of light energy.

The first type of optical guidepath uses fluorescent tape to stripe the floor. The vehicle has an ultraviolet light source to illuminate the stripe, and a photocell sensor that follows the fluorescent light and senses whether the vehicle is straying from the illuminated line. If the vehicle begins to stray off the guidepath, the on-board controller makes steering corrections to keep the vehicle on the guidepath. These systems are sensitive to ambient light, direct sunlight, dirt, and damage of the fluorescent tape. Problems can also result when the background color of the floor changes, thus changing the reflective characteristics. If the fluorescent tape cannot reflect the vehicle's light source, the photocells will lose contact with the guidepath and the vehicle will shut down.

The second method of optical guidepath is stimulated emission of light energy, patented by Litton[1]. Because these guidepaths use fluorescent particles mixed in a liquid substance that can be painted on the floor, they are commonly referred to as chemical guidepaths. The vehicle's scanning head stimulates these particles with ultraviolet

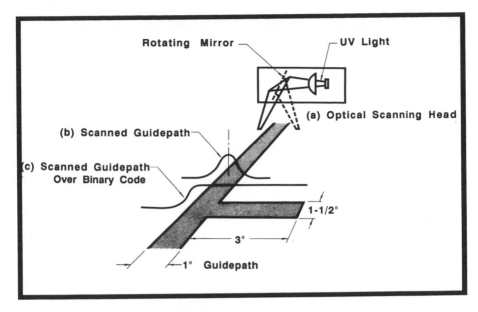

Figure 4.6 Litton's Ultra-Flex™ optical guidance: a) Optical scanning head is made up of an oscillating mirror, photo diode, and a lens. b) The head sees the scanned guidepath as a bell curve. c) Three-inch spurs of guidepath material are applied perpendicular to the guidepath to form binary codes to control the vehicle. (Courtesy of Litton Industrial Automation, Hebron, Kentucky)

light. At the same time, the stimulated portion of the guidepath is scanned to collect the resulting light energy emissions (Figure 4.6 a). The head sees the scanned area as a bell curve—a bright stripe with increasing darkness beyond the edges (Figure 4.6 b). The microprocessor continuously calculates the steering commands necessary for the vehicle to stay on center (maintain a normal curve). Ambient light and floor conditions have very little effect on this type of guidepath.

Vehicles can be designed to bridge five-inch breaks in the optical guidepath, thus preventing the vehicles from shutting down on sections of guidepath that need repair. The cost of installing an optical guidepath is approximately $4.00 per foot.

The optical guidepath can also incorporate codes. Three-inch spurs of guidepath material are applied perpendicular to the guidepath (Figure 4.6 c) to form binary codes to control the vehicle. As the vehicle passes over a code, the head recognizes the spurs when the normal bell curve is interrupted by a straight line of brightness to one side. The binary codes are used to identify guidepath locations, to signal the vehicle to perform auxiliary functions such as sounding the horn or activating a transmitter, and to stop the vehicle.

Guidepath brightness should be monitored, and when the brightness deteriorates the guidepath must be renewed. Most systems last a year or more before renewal is necessary. The renewal process, called refreshing, consists of applying a fresh coat of chemical fluid over the existing guidepath and codes. This process can be completed in one working shift in most installations.

The three main limitations of the passive guidepath are 1) keeping the guidepath, optical sensor, or chemical sensors clean, 2) keeping the focal length between the sensor and guidepath constant, and 3) keeping the guidepath from breaking due to normal wear in high traffic areas.

Recent developments have enabled the passive guide-path to be used in industrial applications as well as clean environments. Improved sensors overcome the sensitivity of the focal length, and improved guidepath materials reduce the wear of the reflective material. More time is required, however, to prove the durability of this technology in dirty industrial environments.

Metal tape can be used as a passive guidepath, with metal detectors as sensors. The metal guidepath tapes are made from stainless steel and are resistant to water, cleaning agents, alkaline solutions, etc. The tape can be mounted on the surface of the floor or can be mounted beneath carpet, tile and other floorings. It can be detected through paint, paper, and accumulated dirt. If the tape is mounted on the floor surface and there is heavy traffic crossing the tape, the metal tape usually is sealed with any of the floor coatings for additional protection. When metal tape is used, durability is less of a concern and maintenance is minimal; vehicles can bridge tape breaks of six to ten inches. Metal code strips can also be incorporated in the guidepath to identify guidepath locations, to signal the vehicle to perform auxiliary functions such as sounding the horn or activating a transmitter, and to stop the vehicle. The cost of installing a metal tape guide-path is $7.00 to $8.00 per foot.

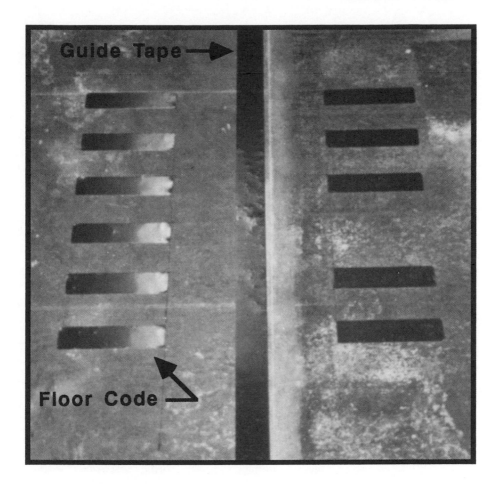

Figure 4.7 TransLogic's Transcar vehicle's patented guidance system follows a passive stainless steel guide tape. Tape can be installed under carpet or tile. Carpet squares provide easy access for expanding and changing the route. Floor codes made from the same tape are used by the vehicles as people use highway signs when driving cars. (Courtesy of TransLogic Corporation, Denver, Colorado)

3-D Tracking System

An alternative guidance system is a 3-D tracking system, such as a beacon system, inertial navigation system, or vision systems. These systems derive their location from known reference points. Beacon systems scan reflective targets to determine vehicle location. Inertial navigation

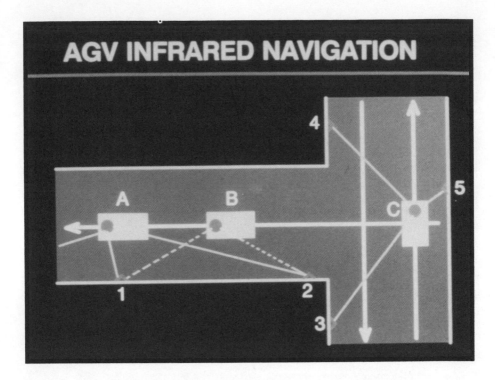

Figure 4.8 AGV Infrared Navigation Vehicle Laser scans reflective targets; on-board vehicle controller uses these known reference points to derive vehicle location. (Courtesy of Caterpillar Industrial, Mentor, Ohio)

systems determine vehicle location from gyroscopes. Vision systems locate recognized images to determine vehicle location. All 3-D tracking systems are expensive and have been used in selective industrial applications. The thrust for developing a 3-D tracking system that requires no guidepath is the desire to use AGVs in applications where laying guidewires is impractical or where electromagnetic fields make wire guidance impossible. These systems are well suited for wood block floors because surface irregularities do not affect them.

To understand how a 3-D system works, compare it to a human being. When a human navigates, he scans the landscape and uses stationary objects as reference. As the human advances along his path, he continually changes his reference points and makes in-course corrections.

The vehicle guidance system works in the same way. Vehicle scanners locate identifiable landmarks (bar code targets) to triangulate the vehicle position. As the vehicle advances it continually scans for different landmarks, and from these reference points it determines its relative position. Landmarks are set every 30 to 50 feet. In between landmarks the vehicle uses measuring wheel technology to dead reckon its navigation. If the vehicle cannot locate a landmark, it will travel a specific distance, generally the maximum distance the vehicle can reliably use measuring wheel technology—30 feet. At this point the vehicle will stop and report to the traffic controller that it needs assistance.

The advantage of 3-D systems is that they don't require a guidepath cut in the floor. The guidepath is replaced with a coordinate system, and the vehicle has the intelligence to navigate the plant layout. Each vehicle has in its on-board controller a map of the coordinates for aisles and P&D stations. The navigation is then done by the vehicle.

Many plants that have an application for AGVs cannot accommodate a buried wire path because of metal objects in the floor, or want a guidepath that is temporary. Using this system, the manufacturer doesn't have to worry about installing more guidepath when changes are necessary. The 3-D tracking represents a truly flexible system, with changes made in the software that controls the AGV, not in the guidepath. Thus, if a P&D station has to be moved one inch, only a simple software change is needed. Furthermore, the 3-D tracking allows the vehicle's route to be expanded or revised with fewer physical changes and at a lower cost than for other guidepath systems.

The limitation of 3-D tracking systems is the sensitivity of the sophisticated electronic equipment, gyroscopes, laser scanners, etc. The electronic equipment requires recalibration because of equipment drifting, and vibration of the vehicles under normal operation. Also, some vision systems are limited in the speed with which they can recognize images. The cost of inertial navigation systems and vision guidance systems is high and makes these systems difficult to justify.

Beacon guidance systems are only now being introduced for standard industrial applications. These vehicles have

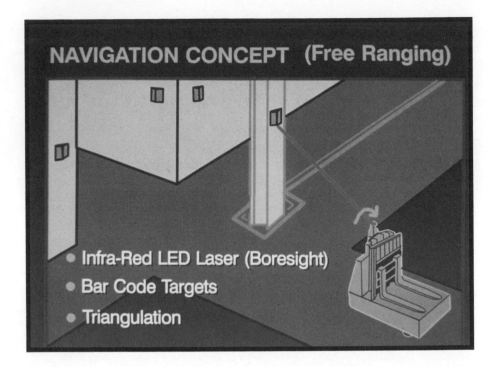

Figure 4.9 Free-ranging vehicle uses low power laser scanning of bar code targets combined with advanced dead reckoning techniques to navigate the factory floor. No buried wires or stripes on the floor are needed. (Courtesy of Caterpillar Industrial, Mentor, Ohio)

been referred to as self-guided vehicle systems (SGVS). They use a laser scanner that searches for reflective bar code targets fixed to the building structure and factory walls. All the target locations are stored in the vehicle's on-board microprocessor to provide tracking reference. The laser sensors provide detailed information, indicating the presence and the position of the target. The laser triangulates off any three targets to determine its precise location at P&D stations, and any two points to navigate along a path; knowing the vehicle location, the controller can navigate the vehicle through the factory. Path changes are a matter of entering software commands and adding bar code targets.

Grid Guidepaths

The grid guidepath is based on the vehicle being able to self-navigate over the entire working area, using a work area map and measuring wheel technology. These guidepaths are laid out in a rectangular coordinate system: a grid or checkerboard pattern. In each corner of the checkerboard a code device is placed, forming the grid pattern. The vehicle reads a code device to know its exact location and can then dead reckon, by measuring wheel technology, to its next location.

The grid pattern is written in software to the vehicle traffic controller. The work area map is stored in the on-board vehicle controller and contains positions of all known obstructions on the grid, such as walls, P&D stations, machines, racks, etc. All possible traffic routes are also stored in the traffic controller.

Inductive Guidepaths

The majority of AGV systems use inductive guidance. The reliability of inductive guidance systems is excellent, providing long life with little or no maintenance when properly installed. Vehicles' ability to accurately track the guidepath depends on a proper installation. For best results there should not be many metallic objects located in the vicinity of the guidepath. It's possible to move or add guidepath with an inductive system, but the floor must be recut and the new guidewires spliced into the existing system. Depending on the size of the change, this can be a time-consuming project.

The guidepath provides vehicle routes, defined by a network of wire loops embedded in sealed grooves cut into the floor. Generally three to six guidepath frequencies are required for complex system layouts, so vehicles can travel independently between addresses on the travel route continually. The on-board vehicle controls choose the correct guidance frequencies to follow at junctions, spurs, etc. without reference to the central control.

Guidepaths are divided into two parts, primary path and secondary path. The traffic flows one way on a primary path, which is identified by reference cross wire and is described by data tables in the computer for traffic control.

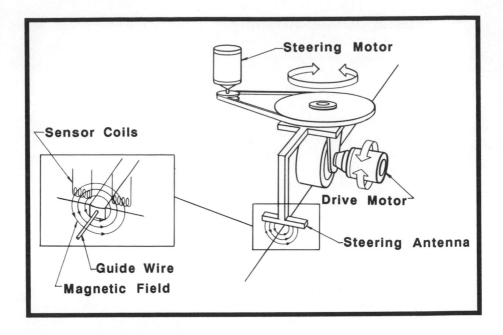

Figure 4.10 *The magnetic field in the inductive guidepath is sensed and followed by the vehicle steering control, consisting of two coils which make up the steering antenna.*

Secondary paths branch off from the primary path and allow traffic to flow in both directions, so vehicles can pick up or drop off material and then reverse direction to return to the primary path.

The guidewire is energized with an alternating current of a specific frequency, producing a concentric magnetic field above the guidepath which can be detected by antennas on the vehicle. If the vehicle strays from the center of the guidewire, the on-board control makes a steering adjustment to correct the vehicle direction. Several low frequencies, ranging from 5-30 kHZ, are transmitted through these wires. In addition, guidewire calibration points are located throughout the system by cutting cross wires in the guidepath network. These reference points are particularly useful if the vehicle uses measuring wheels to determine its exact position between references.

One frequency is for the main guidepath, and the remaining frequencies are used to direct the vehicle through an intersection to travel a different course. These frequencies are routed from intersection to intersection using a secondary slot, making slot cutting more involved than just cutting the main guidepath.

Guidepath wires are commonly 16 or 18 gauge wire and can all be placed in one groove (floor cut), then routed differently throughout the system. The ends of the guidewire loops are connected to frequency generators, used to generate different frequencies under steady state conditions. Depending on the number of frequencies required, more than one generator may be used. The vehicle's steering control unit is equipped with adjustable receiving circuits which are individually tuned to the generator frequencies. The frequency generator is located on the factory floor, generally attached to a building column. Conservatively, one frequency generator is required for every 5000 feet of floor wire. A communication wire may be laid in the same groove as the guidewire, or combined with a guidewire. This communication wire is used to communicate with all vehicles.

Each step in the installation of a guidepath takes time: stenciling the guidepath on the floor before cutting, actually cutting the floor, laying the correct wires in the correct grooves, debugging the guidepath, and finally epoxying and sealing. The cost of installing a guidepath wire is $12 to $20 per foot.

A guidepath layout is drawn to show each guidepath wire and any communication wires, with the frequency and the wire location. This drawing shows how the wiring is connected, and can be of use when identifying and repairing breaks in the guidewire, or installing other machinery. If not properly installed, guidewires can fail years after the system has been commissioned. Care is also required when putting new machinery and components in the floor. Maintenance people anchoring equipment often accidentally cut the wires. The guidepath drawing should be used as a reference to avoid this.

Some vendors have developed special control systems that enable vehicles to follow a square-cut guidepath. The on-board vehicle control interpolates the corners as a standard radius turn. When the vehicle approaches an intersection to make a turn, it passes a floor reference point and begins making the turn before the intersection. Using dead reckoning, it leaves the guidepath, searches for and finds the intersecting guidepath, and continues to its destination. The radius of the turn is predetermined and set in software that controls the vehicle. This technique makes the guidepath easier to cut, reducing the time and expense of installation.

Floor Cutting The floor is cut for an inductive guidance system with a special dust-free, water-cooled, diamond-blade saw. A wet/dry vacuum is used to clean the groove and cutting area. The size of the floor grooves depends on the number of wires to be laid; they generally range from 1/4" to 3/8" wide, and 3/4" to 1-3/4" deep. The floor cut should be wide enough for the wires to lie in the bottom of the groove.

After the wires are laid in the groove, a special profile Styrofoam or sponge rubber rope is placed over them and the groove is filled flush with epoxy resin. It is important that the rope is elastic and has a diameter larger than the crack width. The rope must seal the root of the groove and the wires from the floor compound (epoxy). The open space between the root of the groove and the rope allows the wire to float as the floor shifts, expands, contracts, and settles.

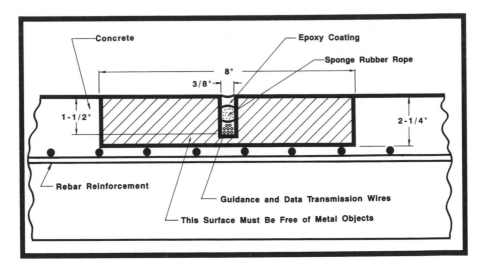

Figure 4.11 Cross section of a concrete floor illustrating the proper installation of the inductive guidepath wire into the floor.

Without this space the wire would break and have to be repaired. Moreover, if changes or additions to the system are necessary, only the top epoxy layer is remolded, leaving the wires undamaged and in the groove.

In buildings with a second floor, the deflection of the floor can harm the wires in the groove, causing premature failures; this is prevented if the wires float. If the groove is too narrow, the wires will be stacked and won't have room to float. The rope won't properly seal the groove, and the sealing compound is likely to stick the wires together and to the sides of the groove. This keeps the wires from floating and leads to premature failures.

When the floor is cut for curves, or groove mergers, the grooves become too wide for the sponge rubber rope to seal. To prevent the sealing compound from getting on the wires, silica sand is used to fill the space between the wire and the rope seal. During installation, the floors are cut and the wires placed in the groove. The final sealing compound must not be used until after the system has been fully checked out, including operating vehicles on the guidepath. Otherwise the installation crew may prematurely seal the floor and have to recut it later, leading to additional project costs, lost project time, and a dissatisfied customer.

Automatic Guidepath Selection for Inductive Guidepaths Complex guidepaths require sophisticated control systems, so vehicles can follow alternate paths at intersections. The controls must select the right path, enabling the vehicle to travel alternate routes to any location on the guidepath in optimum time.

Path selection can be accomplished two ways. The first way, "path switching selection," was the original method used for vehicles following alternate paths. The guidepath is switched on and off by a local controller. The second way, using a less intelligent floor, is "frequency selection." The vehicle selects the guidepath to follow to the proper location. This method is more popular; it is cheaper to install, cheaper to maintain, and is used by most vendors using inductive guidepaths.

In the path switching selection method, a separate floor control system turns sections of the guidepath on and off to direct the vehicle to its correct location. These systems generally use just one guidepath frequency, requiring less floor cutting and wiring. As the vehicle approaches an intersection, it passes a reference point that indicates the vehicle's location. A reed switch then turns on the correct guidepath or turns off the additional path at the intersection. The guidepath the vehicle must follow remains on while the other guidepaths at the intersection are turned off until the vehicle clears the intersection. The vehicle then travels to the next decision point, where it communicates to the reed switch control which path it wants to follow based on its final destination.

One advantage of path switching selection is that it helps prevent vehicles from colliding, because only one vehicle can travel on a guidepath segment at a time.

One of the major disadvantages of this method is that the vehicle must completely clear the intersection before another vehicle can approach the same intersection. In addition, these guidepaths are more complicated, require more maintenance, and are not as reliable. They are used less than the frequency selection method.

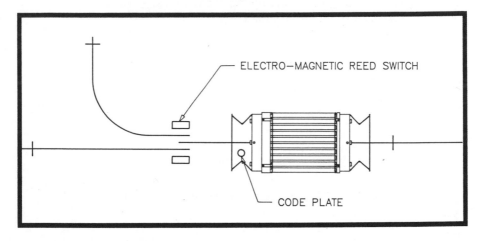

ELECTRO—MAGNETIC REED SWITCH

CODE PLATE

Figure 4.12 As the vehicle branches to another path, it passes over a code element that provides location information to the vehicle. If the vehicle wants to take a new path, its on-board electromagnet trips a reed switch in the floor. This signals the floor controller to energize the appropriate path and de-energize the current path. The floor controller looks for certain conditions prior to energizing the forward path. One of those conditions is the existence of other vehicles. This eliminates vehicle collisions. (Courtesy of Roberts Corporation, Lansing, Michigan)

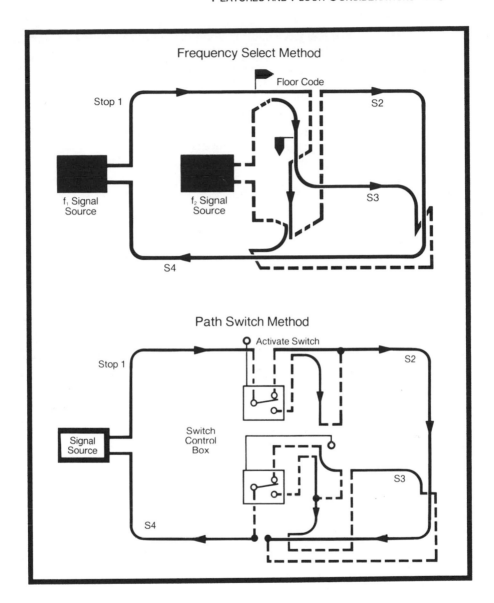

Figure 4.13 These are the inductive guidepath methods used for vehicle routing. The frequency selection method relies on the vehicle to select the proper guidepath to follow, and the path switch method relies on the floor controls to select the proper guidepath for the vehicle to follow. (Courtesy of Gary Koff, Mannesmann Demag, Grand Rapids, Michigan)

Frequency selection is the most common method used in AGV systems; it can more efficiently control the vehicle. As a vehicle approaches an intersection, it passes a reference point that indicates the vehicle's location. From this reference the vehicle knows the correct frequency to follow through the intersection. Each intersection may have several frequencies, used to assist the vehicle in changing routes. At the decision point one guidance frequency goes straight and the other leads to the alternate route. These transitional frequency wires are used only at intersections. They are routed out of the main guidepath slot to a secondary slot and routed to other intersections. The secondary floor slots require additional floor cutting.

The vehicle selects a guidance frequency when it makes its routing decision, and continues to follow that frequency until the instructions are changed. All frequencies are on constantly; the vehicle will not acknowledge any frequency it's not instructed to follow. Multiple frequencies are generally found at guidepath intersections. At other sections of the guidepath, only one frequency is required.

Summary

The correct guidance method depends on the application and the industrial environment. Generally wire-guided systems are the most popular because they are reliable, have been used in many industrial applications, and can accommodate heavy traffic and dirty environments. This track record means the inductive guidepath will probably not be totally replaced by the newer navigation systems.

Systems using optical stripes are less expensive, easier to install and to change, but have problems with mechanical wear of the stripes in high traffic areas and in dirty environments. These systems are found in well-lighted, clean environments and have not been used as extensively as inductive guidepaths.

The direction of guidepath technology has not been totally established. There appears to be a trend toward sophisticated navigation systems, but the newer technology has not proved that it can be economically installed in the typical industrial application. The higher cost of these systems can be partly overcome by not having to put the guidance system in the floor. This system would produce the ultimate in guidepath flexibility, enabling the guidepath to change through software.

Another possible direction is toward simpler passive floor guidance with a sophisticated traffic control on-board the vehicle. This combination allows the use of the simpler, more flexible guidepath. More sophisticated software has been developed for the on-board traffic control; the trend is to reduce hardware and use more software.

FLOOR RAMPS

Ramp applications require special controls to regulate the speed of the vehicle as it descends the ramp. Vehicles can travel on ramps of up to 10% grade with a reduced capacity under normal circumstances. Above a 10% grade, special design is necessary. In systems that use ramps, two vehicles should never be allowed on the ramp at the same time.

An important consideration is the ability of the vehicle to stop while traveling down the ramp. This is not difficult for unit load vehicles; however, AGV trains use individual brakes on each trailer. As the train travels down the ramp the trailer brakes are automatically applied, providing the necessary deceleration for safe traveling. The length of the ramp is important; long ramps can cause overheating of the vehicle's drive motor. A general rule is that a 5% grade ramp will consume twice the power as a vehicle traveling on level ground.

One additional limitation of AGVs traveling on ramps is the vehicle bumper. The bumpers have typically less than 1" of ground clearance; therefore, as the AGV starts up the ramp, the bumper can drag on the ground. Special bumpers and ground clearance must be considered for all AGV systems that include ramps.

Figure 4.14 This AGV, designed to operate indoors and outdoors, moves loads between buildings. The AGV activates a stop light, crosses the street following the guidepath, and moves up a ramp into the next building. (Courtesy of Eaton-Kenway, Salt Lake City, Utah)

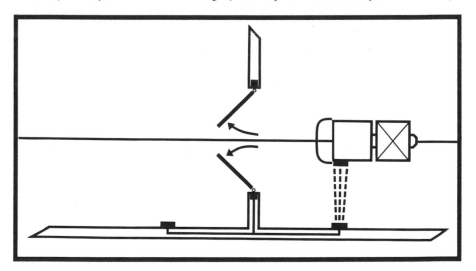

Figure 4.15 Doors in buildings must automatically open to allow the vehicle to pass through and close after the vehicle passes through. Doors can be activated by the vehicle through a sensor.

Figure 4.16 TransLogic Interchangeable Transcar serves multi-floor facilities by automatically calling and entering freight elevators. Communication to the vehicles is through a ceiling-mounted infrared communication box. This box is wired to the system control center and is interfaced with the elevator control system. (Courtesy of TransLogic Corporation, Denver, Colorado)

DOORS/ELEVATORS

Doors in the system must automatically open before the vehicle reaches the door and close after the vehicle passes through. The automatic opening and closing of the door is controlled by a floor switch, photoelectric sensor, or communication loop. The door position (open or closed) is monitored by a limit switch. When the vehicle approaches the door, the control device is activated, the door opens, and the vehicle passes through. Beyond the door, the vehicle passes over a second control device that closes the door. The ideal case is for the door to be opened early enough to allow the vehicle to pass through without stopping.

Using this same type of control, AGVs can be integrated with elevators, allowing them to be used in multi-story buildings.

FLOOR DESIGN

The floor is an important transportation medium and an important part of the material handling system. Everything in the plant sits on it, the vehicles roll on it, rack and conveyors are connected to it, and the guidewires run through it. Careful selection of the floor and floor surface can minimize maintenance problems. Few manufacturing plants have ideal floor conditions. The floors must be studied to determine if the vehicles can be designed to compensate for slightly uneven, greasy, or oily floors.

AGV vendors will specify the gradients, flatness, the tolerances of sub-floor steel, appropriate floor coating resins, and other floor conditions necessary for optimum material handling operation. The user should invite the AGV vendor to inspect and survey the proposed area to approve the floor where the AGV system is to be installed. This survey should include several floor borings to determine its thickness, which will vary considerably. The floor should also be inspected for dusting and exposed aggregate; this condition may indicate weak concrete. If reworking of the floor is required, the AGV vendor should be asked to do the rework, or supervise the rework, and definitely approve the rework when it is completed. It is important to get this approval before the installation of the system. The potential work and cost involved in complying with these conditions should not be underestimated by the end user. Depending on the work required, the cost of preparing the floor can represent up to 25% of the AGV system cost. Adverse floor conditions can cause the best of systems to become inoperable.

Most vehicles require flat floors, varying only 1/4 inch in 10 feet, simply to maintain wheel traction over all parts of the guidepath. But with the advent of high throughput, high lift, automatic material handling equipment (ASRS, AGVS, high lift fork trucks), this traditional standard has been found unsatisfactory. The equipment can operate, but not at optimum performance. This has resulted in the need for both floor levelness and floor flatness specifications.

In the past, floor flatness was a matter of contractor judgement. Now it has become important to prevent waviness in the floor, commonly referred to as the wash-board effect. Too-wavy floors can cause stability problems as the vehicle travels, and may cause the steering antennas to lose contact with the floor.

Floor levelness is required because of the rigid vehicle frame construction, where the supporting wheels could place the driving wheel over a depression and lose traction. If the vehicle travels over a depression, the communication antenna or steering antenna may lose contact, stopping the vehicle or preventing a message from being received. The tolerance on the floor is especially important on a high lift system. When AGV fork vehicles are used, and the lifting height is greater than ten feet, special care must be given to the flatness of the floor. A vehicle lifting a load ten feet or more needs to be level to prevent any problems with load stability.

Floor flatness and levelness have been studied and the F-number system has been developed to address both these issues. The system assigns a numerical value to both levelness and flatness; the larger the number, the better the floor. ASTM (American Society for Testing and Materials) adopted in January, 1988, Standard Test E-1155, "Standard Test Method for Determining Floor Flatness and Levelness Using the F Number System."

It's also important to check the floor contents. If floor reinforcement is used, the distance from the top of the reinforcing bars to the floor surface is critical. The first 1-1/2" to 2-1/4" of the floor must be free of metal heating pipe, metal drains, rebar reinforcement, steel expansion joints, and embedded railroad tracks. Any surface steel thicker than one inch could affect inductive guided vehicles. In addition, any high voltage cables running underground through the building should be identified to the AGV vendor; high voltage cable can cause too much electric interference for a vehicle to operate. The guidepath should be set back ten feet from broad-spectrum noise generators, such as arc welders.

Floor surface must be high-quality, industrial type with resistance to abrasion and wear. Resistance to wear is achieved by use of a high-strength, dense concrete, made with a hard aggregate. The density of concrete should be in the area of 250 pounds per cubic foot. The upper surfaces of the floor should be a hard abrasion-resistant concrete, providing adequate abrasion resistance to vehicle traffic, and impervious to acid and oil spills. Shake-on hardeners are used to toughen floors. If the correct surface is not used, this will lead to noticeable wear in heavy traffic regions.

Floor surface should be a brush surface having a 0.6 coefficient of friction between the floor and the vehicle drive wheel(s). This provides sufficient traction for the AGV to start, turn, and brake. If this coefficient of friction cannot be maintained, slower speeds or resurfacing may be required.

Concrete floors are the best surface for AGV systems; however, systems have been installed on wood block, wood parquet, asphalt surfaces, tile floors, and rough floors such as those found in steel mills. Special installation precautions are required for these surfaces. Wood block floors have grade irregularities and cause problems for vehicles tracking inductive guidepaths; asphalt floors cannot hold up under heavy traffic in hot weather so the vehicle creates ruts in the path and the guidepath eventually breaks. Parquet and tile floors do not have a high enough coefficient of friction for proper traction, so the safe operating speed of the vehicle has to be reduced. All floors except concrete floors have compromises.

Vehicles with neoprene wheels can cause a buildup of static electricity on some floors. When discharged, the static electricity can damage the on-board electric components. This problem can be lessened by equipping vehicles with a ground strap so they can discharge at the floor splices, or when coming in contact with the P&D stands.

PALLETS

The load-carrying function of the vehicle is performed by the pallet, on which components are placed. Pallets must be light, able to carry machined and non-machined components, and have accurate and repeatable dimensions. The most common pallet size is 48" by 40". The pallets can be made from a number of materials, including plastic, metal, molded wood, and wood planks. To determine the optimum pallet for a given application, a pallet analysis can be done by William Sardo, Jr., Pallet and Container Research Laboratory, at Virginia Polytechnic Institute in Blacksburg, Va. The fee for each pallet analysis is approximately $100.

REFERENCES

1) Litton Industrial Automation Publication, *Ultra-Flex Guidance System*, Publication Number SP-101-UFX, August 1986, Litton Industrial Automation, Hebron, Kentucky.

Figure 5.1 FMC AGV Safety Features: This photo shows the major safety features incorporated into a fork vehicle. (Courtesy of FMC Corporation, Material Handling Systems Division, Chalfont, Pennsylvania)

5 SAFETY & WARNING DEVICES

   The safety concerns of the new AGV technology should not be underestimated; they have become a much larger issue than expected, particularly where the vehicles and people work in the same area. During the operation of an AGV system, the safety of the people working with the vehicles and surrounding equipment is paramount. New uses for AGVs demand new ideas on the safety devices incorporated into the system. At the same time, standards are increasing to provide better regulation. Although systems are safer, there is more work to be done.

   In the manufacturing environment, Pareto's 80/20 rule applies to industrial safety. Approximately 20% of the work force is involved in material handling and 80% of the accidents are related to some form of material handling. With this type of record the safety aspects of a material handling system cannot be taken lightly. The buyer of the system should never assume that the vendor considered all the safety aspects of the system; the buyer must doublecheck all precautions.

Safety is emphasized in AGV system design because AGVs are unmanned and appear to be unprotected. They are not like stand-alone equipment, which is self-contained and can be fenced in, so people can't approach the equipment. AGVs travel throughout the plant, interfacing with other equipment and people. As the number of AGVs increases, the risk of an accident increases.

But AGVs have excellent safety records because of standard safety and warning devices and the high level of computer control. The vehicles travel at a controlled speed, following a defined path, with visual and audible warning devices. Most vehicles have safety sensors to stop the vehicle if any objects get in its path. First-time users, however, generally don't consider the system as safe as manually operated forklifts until after it is in operation and the people become confident in the system, paying less attention to the perceived hazards. Moreover, good safety systems increase operators' confidence, helping the acceptance of AGVs in the factory environment.

The safety systems that protect people must be fail-safe and must not depend on the worker protecting himself. The safety devices must also protect the AGVs from themselves. This can be achieved primarily through good traffic management plus reliable anti-collision devices. These two items can often be justified based on the high cost of mechanical repairs, vehicle downtime, and disruption to the material handling system.

Safety needs to be an integral part of AGV system planning; it cannot be an afterthought. No specification is complete without an understanding of the safety requirements for the application and the equipment. In planning a safe system, the following items need to be considered[1]:

- Layout
- Lighting
- Interfacing traffic
- Warning signals
- Emergency systems
- Operational contingencies
- Integrity of the computers
- Security of load

Hazards that must be considered include silent running, unexpected starts, man/machine interface, collision with other vehicles, and proximity of the route to fixed objects, building columns, ancillary machinery, etc[1]. To counteract these common hazards, there are five basic types of safety mechanisms:

VISUAL WARNINGS

These include flashing lights and strobe lights on the vehicle. A strobe produces a flash of light that is highly noticeable, even to persons working in aisles perpendicular to the direction of travel of the vehicle. It informs nearby personnel of the vehicle's presence. Rotating red lights can be used for a similar effect. Occasionally, supplementary warning lights are permanently mounted on the building and overhead and turned on to alert workers when a vehicle is approaching.

Warning signs should be used on the vehicle, in the operating area, and at all entrances to alert anyone entering the area that AGVs are in operation.

The AGV and the machinery on it are often painted different colors, depending on the motion of the attached equipment. Orange is used to designate dangerous parts on the AGV that can cut, crush, or cause other injuries. This color is also used on guarding that covers a hazard. Yellow designates caution and marks hazards such as pinch points, tripping, and striking. This color coding is used on assembly vehicles that have constant interaction with people.

Aisles used by AGVs should be clearly marked, with stripes painted on the floor to show exactly where the vehicle travels. This safety feature helps people and AGVs work in the same area. Otherwise a person may be standing out of the proper path of the vehicle, or what he recognizes to be the proper path, and the vehicle may move outside of the perceived path and approach the person. This can occur on curves where vehicles oversteer to straighten out.

Figure 5.2 An example of a warning sign used to alert truck and car traffic of AGV operating in the area. (Courtesy of Eaton-Kenway, Salt Lake City, Utah)

Figure 5.3 Demag/Barrett Model AGV-240C, bi-directional unit load vehicle with a powered lift/lower deck, operating in an automotive stamping plant. Note the contrast of the painted floor. This shows people working in the area where the vehicles travel and where the guidepath is located. The guidepath is striped and the protected area where a vehicle travels is painted a solid color. (Courtesy of Mannesmann Demag, Grand Rapids, Michigan)

AUDIBLE WARNINGS

An audible warning is used to alert people working in an area of various operating and emergency conditions. The warning usually sounds just before the vehicle moves, and as it travels along the guidepath. This signal can be either a mechanical warning bell or an electronic beeper. The warning device should be loud enough to be easily heard above the ambient noise. Some electronic beepers can be programmed to make independent sound patterns and can be made to play a short tune as the warning signal.

AREA RESTRICTIONS

Areas where it may be difficult to protect people can be isolated. It is possible to stop people entering floor areas by the use of fencing, pressure sensitive mats, or light curtains at entrances. The only absolute way to make sure people are not in a restricted area is by visual inspection.

Careful path planning and layout is important in the safety of the system; areas where people might get trapped and crushed must be identified. Transfer stations where AGVs interface with other moving equipment must be carefully installed to ensure that the people working in these areas are protected.

At least 18 inches should be maintained between the vehicles and any columns or obstructions. If a potential pinch point of less than 18 inches exists, it should be identified and marked. This is particularly critical on turns or through doorways. The vehicle must not travel so close to an object that its slow-down sensor detects the object and forces the vehicle into the slow-down mode. If this is a recurring event, it can cause inefficiencies in the system.

In systems that use ramps, two vehicles should never be allowed on a ramp at the same time.

Speed Control

Speed control is important to the safe and reliable operation of an AGV. If the throughput requirements are too demanding and require the vehicle to move at excessive speeds, load stability problems can result. An example of this would be a quick 90-degree turn that causes the load to shift. If the load shifts during the handling process, the vehicle is stopped and the load must be repositioned. A vehicle approaching a curve should travel through the curve at a reduced speed to prevent the load from shifting or the vehicle from traveling off the guidepath.

The maximum speed of the AGV varies with the type of AGV and the application. The normal pressure of automated material handling is to produce more: a higher throughput rate, at a reduced cost. This can be easily achieved by increasing the speed of vehicles. However, safety is the main consideration in holding back vehicle speeds in most applications.

Vehicle speeds exceeding 300 feet per minute can be used in applications where the vehicle is totally isolated from people. One of the problems in high speed applications is being able to stop the vehicle within the compression distance of the bumper. In Europe, AGVs working in the same area as people are restricted to one meter per second.

STOPPING SYSTEM

Stopping systems can be divided into two categories, manual and automatic. Manual emergency stops are push buttons located on the vehicle so personnel can stop it in an emergency. These push buttons can be located anywhere on the vehicle chassis; they can be located on all sides of the vehicle. In addition, some vehicles in assembly applications

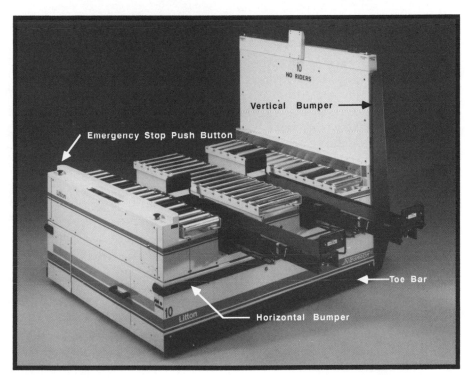

Figure 5.4 Unit Load Integrator™ vehicle with a shuttle transfer device. This vehicle is designed to carry pallet-sized loads up to 4000 pounds to designated pickup and drop-off stations. Included on this vehicle are horizontal and vertical bumpers, toe bar, and four manually activated emergency stop push buttons. (Courtesy of Litton Industrial Automation, Hebron, Kentucky)

have an emergency kick rail or toe bar which wraps around the perimeter of the vehicle, about one inch off the floor, and is activated when pressed by the operator's foot. To deactivate, the rail is pressed a second time.

The vehicles should be designed so that when emergency stop is activated, the load rollers and wheels will still be loaded, preventing tipping. This can be a problem when the AGV is traveling with no load, causing the load rollers to lift off the ground and the vehicle to lose contact with the guidepath.

Automatic stopping systems can be further divided into contact types (emergency bumpers), which require impact before they operate, and non-contact types such as ultrasonic or photo-electric sensors.

Emergency Bumpers

An emergency bumper is a spring-loaded bumper that collapses under impact. The emergency bumpers usually contact the object at a slow speed, and the vehicle comes to an emergency stop in a short distance. Depending on the vehicle's load, the floor surface conditions, vehicle speed, etc., the vehicle stopping distance will vary. Nominally, this distance is 18 to 24 inches. It is important to make sure the vehicle can stop within the compression distance of the bumper. If the vehicle can't do this, the vehicle will hit the obstruction and cause damage or hurt someone.

Emergency bumpers extend beyond the width of a loaded vehicle to provide protection for wide loads the vehicle may transport. Bumpers are located on the front of the vehicle; bi-directional vehicles also have bumpers in the rear.

The impact activates the emergency brake. This emergency braking system, through a direct control circuit, fails to safety under all conditions. A spring-applied brake is used on each drive motor to insure the vehicle stops when electric power is not available. The sensing system must be self-monitoring so that failure of any component, including the sensor itself, results in automatic stopping.

The vehicle braking system must be able to stop the vehicle before it hits an obstacle in its path. A positive brake type is the most widely accepted emergency braking system. It consists of a switch that opens the circuit when the bumper is activated. It should not be possible to start the vehicle until the fault has been corrected. As an added precaution, after the emergency bumpers have been activated, the vehicle must be manually restarted by an operator.

Another type of emergency bumper includes a collision guard that activates a photo eye, which is mounted on the vehicle and is focused on a target on the back of the bumper. When the bumper hits an object, the target distances change, the photo eye senses this change, and it stops the vehicle. One disadvantage is that any bumps in the floor can jar the bumper and stop the vehicle.

Figure 5.5 Roberts' TrakStar Model RTA-105, uni-directional unit load vehicle, equipped with an electro-mechanical tote handling shuttle. Note the vehicle has a foam bumper. (Courtesy of Roberts Corporation, Lansing, Michigan)

Both types of emergency bumper are usually attached to the AGV in a suspended flexible skirt. This design has two limitations: It provides only limited protection along the sides of the vehicle, and it allows people to stand inside the skirt, thus eliminating the protection of this safety feature. This type of bumper is undesirable on assembly AGVs where operators will be standing close to the vehicle to do their assembly task.

Tactile bumpers don't have the above limitations. Made from a solid sponge-like material, these soft bumpers sense contact over less than an inch of bumper depression and shut down the vehicle. These bumpers are popular throughout Europe. The concern is how durable these bumpers are over time.

An optional safety feature is bumpers, side flaps, or sensors on all the sides of the AGV. This can be accomplished by either a small bumper being attached to the sides of the vehicle and along the edge length of the fork, or side flaps being attached to the sides of the vehicle. If these bumpers are contacted the vehicle will go into an emergency

Figure 5.6 Demag/Barrett Model AGV-140L, bi-directional unit load vehicle, equipped with a powered roller deck for handling bag products. Maximum load capacity of this vehicle is 4000 pounds. Note the extended side safety flaps, which extend beyond the vehicle body, used to protect the powered roller deck, which also extends past the vehicle body. If contact is made with these flaps, the vehicle comes to a stop. (Courtesy of Mannesmann Demag, Grand Rapids, Michigan)

Figure 5.7 Demag/Barrett Model AGV-240C, bi-directional unit load vehicle, equipped with a powered lift/lower deck, used for transporting a carpet roll up to 9 feet in length and 5 feet in diameter. Unfinished rolls of carpet are picked up at the finished end of the process machines and delivered to the shipping department. Note that the product does not extend past the front and rear bumper. Also, additional warning lights are mounted on the bumper support. (Courtesy of Mannesmann Demag, Grand Rapids, Michigan)

stop condition. These can provide extra protection if the vehicle over-steers in turns.

Sonar and Optical Sensors

These sensors detect potential collisions and instruct the vehicle to slow down and prepare to stop. They project a signal in the front of the vehicle to sense obstacles in its path. One type, an ultrasonic proximity sensor, detects obstacles prior to collision. The vehicle can be designed to either stop

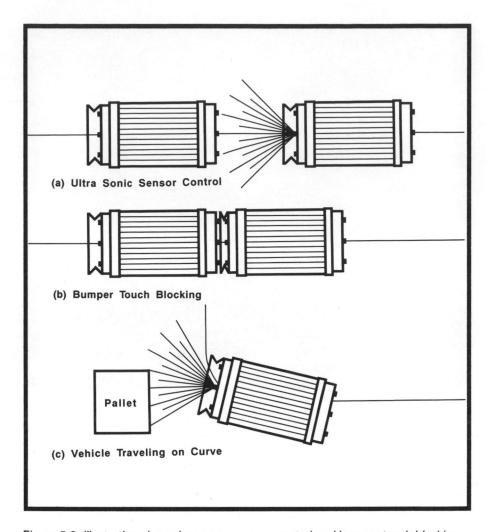

(a) **Ultra Sonic Sensor Control**

(b) **Bumper Touch Blocking**

Pallet

(c) **Vehicle Traveling on Curve**

Figure 5.8 Illustration shows how sonar sensor control and bumper touch blocking function: a) Ultrasonic sensor control detects an object in its path and shifts into slow speed. b) Bumper hits object and shifts into emergency stop. c) Vehicle detects object in its path and shifts into slow speed—object is not actually in the vehicle's path. (Courtesy of Roberts Corporation, Lansing, Michigan)

or continue at reduced speed, allowing the bumper to make gentle contact with the object. The combination of proximity sensors and mechanical bumpers is used on most vehicles.

One problem with the sonar or optical devices is that they may detect an object ahead of the vehicle that is not actually in the vehicle's path. This happens frequently at turns, where objects such as columns or racks appear to be in the vehicle's path—but the vehicle turns before the objects would be encountered. When necessary, vehicle controls can be overridden for conventional manual operation. While it is highly desirable to avoid collisions, it is also necessary to avoid too many false alarms. The sonar and optical sensors are frequently turned off temporarily, or the range can be shortened while the vehicle travels through turns to avoid seeing objects in the detection range of the sensor but not in the path of the vehicle.

Sonar Devices

Sonar devices have a maximum detection range of about 20 feet. For most AGV applications, seven feet is the maximum range required. The sonar beam is approximately a 17-degree cone, which is more desirable than the standard photocell's wider band. A sonar device can also be programmed for a finite number of ranges of protection. For example, when vehicles turn corners, the full seven-foot range is unnecessary, because it would be easy for the vehicle to detect an obstruction outside the guidepath (e.g., columns, etc.). The vehicle instead turns down the range to two feet. The microprocessor on-board the vehicle can be programmed to change the sonar range depending on the speed of the vehicle and any guidepath locations that restrict the width of the band. Sonar devices provide more flexibility, which helps the vehicle cycle through the system faster, by eliminating unnecessary slowdowns.

Photocells

Photocells are light-reflective sensors with a maximum detection range of 40 feet. The beam width on a photocell is typically one foot wide at three feet from the source.

Any interference with the beam puts the vehicle in a slow speed condition. The reflective surface of the obstacle determines the distance at which the photocell can detect it. Typically these sensors can detect an obstruction about three feet on a dark reflective surface and approximately ten feet on a good white reflective surface. This wide range (three to ten feet) is the disadvantage of a photocell. A white surface detected ten feet from the vehicle automatically forces the vehicle to slow down for the full ten feet. Furthermore, photocells don't have separate controllable distance ranges; only one range is available. Therefore, whenever the vehicle enters a corner, it detects objects outside the guidepath and slows down. These disadvantages prevent the vehicle from operating efficiently; the excess slow-speed travel wastes valuable time.

Guidepath Monitor

The guidepath monitor located on the vehicle shuts the vehicle down if it wanders from the guidepath. The wandering tolerance depends on the AGV manufacturer; typically it is less than one inch. This feature prevents the vehicle from travelling when there is no guidepath signal. For example, if the power fails, the guidepath generator stops and the guidepath signal disappears, causing the vehicle to stop.

If a requirement of the AGV system is that the entire system must shut down in an emergency, an easy way to achieve this is by shutting off the guidepath generators. This initiates automatic shutdown of all vehicles.

Conclusion

A final comment on safety: Absolute safety cannot be built into the system. Safe operation is based on a combination of safety devices and, most important, competent operators. All people working within the system must be trained. Thus, it is important to build effective training programs for personnel. This training should cover how the system is to be used, all the safety features that have been built into the vehicles, and the limitations of the system.

Well-trained personnel are an important part of the good safety record of AGVs.

REFERENCES

1) K. Cheshire, "Some Safety Aspects of AGVs," Ford Motor Company Ltd, UK. This paper was presented at the Third International Conference of Automated Guided Vehicles Systems, October 1985, Stockholm, Sweden.

Additional reference which was not used in the book but should be referred to is "Safety Standard for Guided Industrial Vehicles," ASME/ANSI B56.5-1988, published by The American Society of Mechanical Engineers, New York, New York.

Figure 6.1 Demag/Barrett Model AGV-240C unit load vehicle at a battery exchange station. Battery exchange is assisted by an extractor mechanism. Battery chargers are located on the top shelf of the rack, with two shelves used to store batteries during the recharging process. Note the sheet metal air ducts above the battery charging units; these air ducts are used to improve the ventilation in the charging area. (Courtesy of Mannesmann Demag, Grand Rapids, Michigan)

6 BATTERY REQUIREMENTS

The majority of AGVs are powered from batteries on-board the vehicle. These batteries drive the vehicle, power the accessory equipment, and provide power for the on-board electronic controls. Thus the batteries and the battery charging systems are extremely important to the overall uptime and efficiency of the AGV system. AGVs usually operate with 12 volt, 24 volt, 48 volt, or 72 volt dc industrial batteries.

There are basically two different types of battery systems used in AGVs. The first type, for material delivery systems, powers the vehicle for several hours before the battery needs to be charged. The second type, for assembly systems, powers the vehicle for only a few minutes before the batteries need to be charged. Each system uses different capacity batteries and type charger. The correct combination of battery capacity and charging unit depends on the application.

Material Delivery Vehicles

For material delivery systems, battery capacities typically range from 200 to 500 amp-hours. The capacity required in most applications seldom exceeds 800 amp-hours. The battery capacity of a vehicle depends on how large the vehicle's battery compartments are and the duty cycle requirements. Because batteries are heavy, large, and awkward, they are generally sized for the specific application, with the objective of having enough capacity to last for a predetermined time, usually 8-12 hours. Too much battery in a vehicle can add unnecessary weight, require additional space, and affect vehicle performance.

Battery capacity should be determined based on the vehicle's duty cycle and the system requirements. The amp draw for each movement and function of both a loaded and an unloaded vehicle should be determined. Based on the amp draw figures and the number of times a vehicle is to perform these functions during a given time, the amp-hour battery capacity requirements can be calculated for the application.

These are the general battery capacities for various material delivery vehicles:

Vehicle Type	Amp-Hour Rating*
Driverless trains	400 to 1000
Pallet vehicles	300 to 600
Unit load vehicle	200 to 850
Fork vehicle	300 to 1000
Lightweight vehicles	100 to 300

* Amp-hour rating is at a six-hour rate of discharge.

Battery life of five to six years is not unusual if the batteries are sized right for the application and a good maintenance program is in place for watering, cleaning, and equalizing the battery charge.

Figure 6.2 Control Engineering Company LPV vehicle has a specially designed platform fixture used for carrying sheet metal decks. The vehicles shown in this photo are parked in an automatic charging station. (Courtesy of Control Engineering Company, Harbor Springs, Michigan)

One set of batteries should be used for each eight-hour shift of operation. This provides enough time to charge the batteries and allow the proper cooling. If the vehicle is to be operated during two or more successive shifts, its battery packs have to be changed. Spare batteries are cheaper than additional vehicles to support the system.

An alternative to charging the batteries for a second shift is to charge them when the charge is low or when there is lengthy scheduled idle time. This means the vehicle must have a device for automatic battery charging. Automatic battery charging requires special equipment to be installed in the vehicle, including a recharging device, the appropriate control unit, and the stationary structure to which the vehicle connects for charging. Battery charge status can be displayed on-board the vehicle for manual monitoring.

Almost all AGVs for material delivery systems have low-battery warning systems. Low-battery warning systems extend the life of the battery by indicating when the battery has been discharged, and then returning the vehicle to a charging area so the battery can be recharged. When the battery charge drops to a preset level, the on-board vehicle software instructs the vehicle to finish its current task and then go to the charging area, where the battery is replaced or recharged.

Material delivery systems generally use traction batteries. Discharging the traction batteries more than 80% puts a strain on the battery and shortens its life. Charging traction batteries before they have been 80% discharged will actually shorten the life of the batteries; battery life depends on the number of times the battery is charged. Low battery voltage can cause motors to overheat, leading to ultimate failure or burned relay contacts or other electrical components—and higher costs. Proper care of the batteries will prolong vehicle life by extending the life of the electrical components.

Assembly Vehicles

The assembly vehicle has evolved into a low-profile vehicle, which restricts battery height to approximately 15 inches. Thus these vehicles use low-profile traction batteries or automotive type batteries with a relatively low capacity (amp-hours). Because of the low battery capacity, the vehicles will perform only a few functions or travel a short distance before the batteries need to be recharged. These characteristics require that for assembly applications the battery size and battery charging be carefully reviewed for the application. The typical traction battery life for an assembly application is three to four years; for an automotive type battery, it is considerably less.

For example, assume that a vehicle will draw 250 amps when traveling empty and 470 amps when traveling loaded. If the vehicle speed is 100 feet/minute, the vehicle travels 100 feet in one minute. If the vehicle travels loaded for one minute, the current draw will be 470 amp-minutes or 7.83 amp-hours. For an unloaded vehicle traveling one minute, the current draw will be 250 amp-minutes or 4.16 amp-hours. Assuming the vehicle uses automotive batteries, with a rated capacity of 80 amp-hours, the discharge of the battery before charging would be 8 to 16 amp-hours. Therefore after a loaded vehicle has traveled approximately 100 feet or an unloaded vehicle 200 feet, the battery would need to be recharged. This example illustrates the importance of properly sizing the vehicle's battery capacity to the system requirements, and system layout, and emphasizes the frequency with which batteries need to be recharged.

One point not brought out in the above example is the time required to recharge the batteries. The automotive battery maintains a relatively high charge level, never dropping below 80% before recharging. Because of this high level, any recharging must be done slowly to prevent overheating of the battery. In short, it's time-consuming to recharge the automotive type battery. The rule of thumb is that AGVs travel one-third of the time and are idle two-thirds of the time. During this idle time, the vehicle can be charged. If the specified idle time is less than the two-to-one ratio, more vehicles must be added to the system.

BATTERY TYPES

Lead Acid Automotive Batteries[1]

Automotive batteries are a low-power battery designed for infrequent, high current drains of short duration. The typical automotive battery has a rating of 80 to 100 amp-hours (at a six-hour discharge rate), with the maximum discharge capacity of 20% or 16 to 20 amp-hours; below this point strains the battery and the electrical system. These batteries can be used for light-duty AGV applications or assembly systems that use a frequent charging system, such as opportunity charging. The batteries would be charged after a series of short vehicle movements or lifts. The advantage of this type of battery is that the profile and weight of the vehicle are reduced, and the batteries are cheaper.

Automotive batteries are available either as a standard battery, or a maintenance-free battery. Standard batteries flood the lead plates in the battery with a diluted sulfuric acid; as the batteries are charged and recharged the lost fluid can be replaced with water. A maintenance-free battery is a standard battery with larger fluid capacity and no ability to replace fluid. Both type batteries have the same characteristics and both types will gas to some degree during recharging. The maintenance-free battery uses a low gassing alloy to reduce gassing during the charging process. This type of battery, however, is not recommended for most AGV applications because the battery does not deep discharge (deep cycle) well, the discharge capacity is low, and battery life is limited (experienced with deep cycling).

One of the disadvantages of wet cell batteries is the gassing of batteries when they are charged. The electrode plates inside the battery are submerged in a diluted sulfuric acid commonly referred to as electrolyte. As the batteries are charged they gas, and the gas is vented out the cell caps. After the battery reaches full charge almost all added energy goes in gassing. Since a 4% concentration of hydrogen in the air is explosive, proper ventilation of battery charging areas is required for safety. The gassing point is the point at which bubbling of hydrogen in the electrolyte occurs. The maximum charge rate is set by the maximum allowable temperature rise in the battery's electrolyte and the requirement not to produce excessive gassing. A lead acid battery that has been normally discharged can absorb electrical energy rapidly without overheating or excessive gassing. Normally batteries will start gassing at 80% recharge. The gassing process begins in the range of 2.30 to 2.38 volts per cell, depending on the cell chemistry and construction.

Lead Acid Traction Batteries[1]

Traction batteries, commonly called deep cycle discharge batteries, are designed to be discharged continuously at relatively moderate current drains, with a downward curving discharge characteristic, meaning that the voltage of the battery decreases as it is discharged. These batteries have a long proven record of use in forklift trucks, high energy capacities, and heavy-duty construction. They can obtain capacities up to 1000 amp-hours with the maximum discharge capacity of 80% or 800 amp-hours; below this point strains the battery and the electrical system.

These batteries are designed for a finite number of cycles of discharge and charge; a typical life is 1500 to 2000 cycles at an 80% depth of discharge. The deeper the discharge, the fewer cycles of service.

On completion of an 80% discharge, these batteries should be taken out of service to prevent damage to the battery and the equipment it powers, and recharged in a controlled manner between 105% to 115% of battery capacity. After recharging they are again put into service. The batteries should be restored to a charge between 115% to 125% of battery capacity at least every 30 days to prevent a gradual decline in capacity. These batteries are available as a standard battery or a sealed maintenance-free battery.

Deep-cycle, sealed, maintenance-free batteries provide attractive advantages over standard lead acid traction batteries. These cells use a low gassing alloy and gas-recombination technology to reduce the gassing and effects of corrosive electrolyte, eliminating the need to protect the vehicle and its components from acid vapor. The batteries are cleaner and acid spills are not common. In short, sealed maintenance-free batteries are superior to standard or maintenance-free batteries and are used in most AGV applications.

Overcharging the batteries accelerates gassing, increases water loss, corrodes the positive plates, and shortens the battery life. Overcharging takes place when the battery remains on charge after the equalizing or trickle charge period is finished. This is a typical problem with single setting chargers which use a timer to limit the cycle time. Frequently batteries are overcharged or undercharged, providing no control over the charging process. Furthermore, these chargers do not have automatic charge termination, which would turn the charger off when the battery is fully charged.

Many of the charging problems are a result of the fact that lead acid batteries' ability to accept a charge decreases as the state of charge of the battery increases. This is why lead acid batteries require considerable time to recharge the battery, have overheating problems, and require long cool-down times.

Fiber Nickel Cadmium Batteries[2]

Fiber nickel cadmium batteries are a revolutionary development as applied to AGVs. These batteries are new to the US market, but have been used in Europe since the early 1980s. They were originally developed for an electric powered automobile, but are ideal for AGV applications.

A few advantages of fiber nickel cadmium batteries are:

- Fiber nickel cadmium batteries can be charged 30 times faster than a lead acid battery. This means they can accept charging currents of extremely high rates without the heat buildup common to other types of batteries. It is well known that heat destroys battery plates and reduces battery life. Because of this fast charging rate, the number of battery chargers and floor space required for an AGV system can be reduced, which can be a substantial savings.

  With the use of fiber nickel cadmium batteries the battery charging and exchange rooms will become obsolete. AGV systems that use on-board battery charging with lead acid batteries require significant charging time. In the same application, vehicles using fiber nickel cadmium batteries require less time to recharge, enabling the vehicles to spend significantly more time delivering loads rather than parking at a charging position.

- Compared to lead acid batteries, fiber nickel cadmium batteries for a given application can reduce battery size and weight. For example, an application requiring a 450 amp-hour lead battery may require only a 150 amp-hour fiber nickel cadmium battery. The difference in the requirements to store a 450 amp-hour lead acid battery compared to a 150 amp-hour fiber nickel cadmium battery can be substantial. A rule of thumb: fiber nickel cadmium batteries require one-third the size battery compartments as lead acid batteries and are about one-third the weight. That means the size of the vehicle and the drive motor can also be reduced.

- Fiber nickel cadmium batteries have long life expectancy. Table 6.1 shows the life expectancy as a function of depth of discharge of the battery. For example, a 10% depth of discharge has an expected life of 100,000 cycles. This is equivalent to (3 charges per hour)(8 hour/shift)(2 shift/day)(240 day/year) = 11520 cycles per year or 8.6 years expected life.

- Fiber nickel cadmium batteries can be completely discharged, and then recharged to full capacity without measurable loss of capacity. This type of abuse has been repeated 3000 times without damage to the cells.

The disadvantage of the fiber nickel cadmium battery appears to be its initial cost compared to that of a lead acid battery. But in evaluating the total battery requirements for an AGV system, using fiber nickel cadmium batteries reduces the number of battery chargers, the floor space needed to store spare battery packs, and the number of people to support the charging area. In short, these batteries are not more expensive than a lead acid battery, and in most cases will actually produce a cost savings.

The use of fiber nickel cadmium batteries requires a different thought process. A lead acid battery is best used by taking the battery out of service, charging the battery to full capacity, putting the battery back into service, and repeating the process. Fiber nickel cadmium batteries are charged when the vehicles are doing other work or stopped for other reasons.

Because of the short charging time, the fiber nickel cadmium battery can fully charge to its working capacity at a P&D stand while the vehicle is completing a pickup or delivery, or while the vehicle is in a holding queue waiting for work assignments. It can also be charged as the vehicle passes through a charging section of the guidepath. A charging rail is mounted to the floor alongside the guidepath; as the vehicle passes this section, a charging shoe on the vehicle makes contact with the charging rail. As the vehicle travels along the rail, the battery is being charged. This process eliminates the need for a vehicle to be parked in order to recharge the battery.

The charging time of these batteries is short. After 100% discharge, they can be charged to full operating capacity of 1.55 volts per cell in less than 18 minutes[3] and brought to working capacity in 40 seconds to 3 minutes, depending on the application. Because of this short charging time, a single battery charger can be wired to several charging positions in the system. While the battery charger can charge only one vehicle at a time, many vehicles can be charged with one charger.

Fiber Nickel Cadmium Battery Sizing Formulas and Battery Operating Characteristics

In sizing fiber nickel cadmium batteries, two key principles must be considered: 1) the desired life of the battery for the application, and 2) keeping the CnA ratio (amp rating of the battery charger to the amp-hour rating of the battery) within the recommended ratings.

Table 6.1 is used as the guideline to determine expected life of the battery. This table is based on eight years of field data from Hoppecke Battery Systems in Germany. The end of useful life of a battery was determined when the battery had only 30% of the total capacity remaining. In Table 6.1 the depth of discharge is from the operating capacity of the battery and not the maximum capacity of the battery. Actual on-site tests have demonstrated over twice the expected life (Table 6.1) from these batteries. Ambient temperatures, duty cycle, and depth of discharge of the battery greatly affect its expected life.

TABLE 6.1   BATTERY CHARGING CYCLES

Depth of Discharge	Expected Life
10%	100,000
20%	40,000
30%	27,000
40%	20,000

Table 6.2 is the fiber nickel cadmium battery characteristics for the AGV applications. CnA values above these limits are not necessarily recommended for AGV applications.

TABLE 6.2   RECOMMENDED CnA RATIOS[3]

CnA Ratio	Recharged Capacity of Battery
1.5	92%
1.8	84%
2.0	80%
2.5	67%
3.0	49%

CnA = (Amp rating of the battery charger)/(Amp-hour rating of the battery)

The percentages represent the recharged capacity of the battery to the operating voltage of 1.55 volts per cell; e.g. at 1.5 CnA the battery is recharged to 92% of the total capacity of the battery by the time it reaches the cutoff voltage of 1.55 volts per cell.

When computing the amount of amps that must be returned to the battery, remember that 18% of the recharging amps will be lost due to inefficiencies such as heat. This means that the amps consumed by the battery plus 18% must be added to obtain the total recharging amps needed to recharge the batteries. To make the calculation simple, multiply the CR (capacity to replace) by 1.2. Therefore the charger size (CR) is calculated as follows: CR = (1.20) (AHC), where AHC = Amp-Hours Consumed.

The procedure for determining the method of sizing the fiber nickel cadmium battery and charger is as follows:

Step 1: Determine the battery consumption, for a given period of time, before recharging is required.

Step 2: Calculate the capacity to replace (CR) required to recharge the battery to its working capacity. CR = (1.20) (AHC)

Step 3: Select the desired time required for recharging the battery to its working capacity. RT = Required time for recharging.

Step 4: Calculate the charger size (CS) required to recharge the battery in the desired time limit. CS = CR/RT

Step 5: Determine the depth of discharge (DoD) for the application. As shown in Table 6.1, the depth of discharge depends on the expected life of the battery, and the optimum battery life is obtained at the 10% depth of discharge.

Step 6: Determine the battery size required. Battery size = CR (100/DoD)

Step 7: Calculate the CnA ratio to determine if the battery charger and battery combination are operating in the proper range, shown in Table 6.2. If not, a different size battery charger and battery should be selected.

<u>Example 1:</u> This example illustrates the sizing of a fiber nickel cadmium battery for an opportunity charging AGV system.

Step 1: Assume 25 amp-hour battery discharge before battery charging is required.

Step 2: Charge required to bring battery to working capacity. CR = 1.20 (25) = 30 amp-hours

Step 3: Assume a three-minute time period required to recharge the battery to its working capacity. RT (Required time for recharging) = 3 minutes

Step 4: Charger size required to bring battery to its working capacity within the desired time period. Amp rating of charger = CS = CR/RT. CR/RT = (30 amp-hour) (60 minutes/hour)/3 minutes = 600 amp charger

Step 5: For optimum battery life select a depth of discharge of 10%.

Step 6: Battery size required: CR (100/DoD) = 30 (100/10) = 300 amp-hour

Step 7: CnA = 600/300 = 2   Table 6.2 shows this ratio is within the recommended operating characteristics of the battery, therefore the selected battery size and battery charger is satisfactory.

<u>Example 2:</u> A more typical opportunity charging example.

Step 1: Assume six amp-hour battery discharge before battery charging is required.

Step 2: Charge required to bring battery to working capacity. CR = 1.20 (6) = 7.2 amp-hours

Step 3: Assume a one-minute time period required to recharge the battery to its working capacity. RT (Required time for recharging) = 1 minute

Step 4: Charger size required to bring battery to its working capacity within the desired time period. Amp rating of charger = CR/RT. CR/RT = (7.2 amp-hour) (60 minutes/hour)/1 minute = 432 amp charger. Use a 450 amp battery charger, therefore charging time will be 57.6 seconds.

Step 5: For optimum battery life select a depth of discharge of 10%.

Step 6: Battery size required: CR (10) = 7.2 (10) = 72 amp-hour

Step 7: CnA = 450/72 = 6.25 Table 6.2 shows this ratio is too high and would not be recommended for the battery and battery charger selected. Therefore a new battery and battery charger should be selected.

Step 8: Assume CnA = 2.5, therefore (Charger size)/(CnA) = 450/2.5 = 180 amp-hour battery.

Notice that FNC batteries are charged with constant current, of the full charger amps, regardless of the depth of discharge.

Battery Chargers

Several types of battery chargers are used in AGV systems, including pulse charging, taper charging, two-rate charging, constant current charging, and constant voltage charging. Specifying the charger for the AGV system is not an exact science. There are new developments in battery chargers, and it is suggested that the user be aware of current battery charging technology and be involved with selecting the chargers.

It's the job of the charger to put the power back into the battery in time for the next shift, ideally with time left over for the battery to cool down. A proper battery charger recharges an 80% discharged battery in eight hours in a multi-shift operation or overnight in a single shift operation. Some battery chargers read the discharge condition of the battery and take only the time necessary to recharge it, not exceeding eight hours, and provide trickle charge before shutting off. Attempts to recharge a battery discharged to 80% in less than eight hours often result in excessive heat buildup in the battery. A 480 volt, three-phase charger should be used because of the significant energy efficiency improvement: energy costs are reduced over single-phase equipment.

Usually chargers are matched closely to the amp-hour capacity of the battery and the type of battery—standard or maintenance-free. A smaller charger can be used but takes longer than eight hours to recharge the battery. A higher capacity charger may be used for recharging in fewer than eight hours, but this increases the battery temperature, especially on inner cells of large batteries. Care must be taken not to exceed the battery manufacturer's recommended temperature limits. Whether the battery is standard or maintenance-free is also important in selecting the charger. Each type has different charging characteristics that require different kinds of chargers.

Large AGV systems require several battery chargers. If the charging area is not thought out in detail, the floor space required can become large. To save space, the battery chargers can be mounted overhead.

In addition, the close proximity of the battery charger to computers, both on-board the AGV and off-board, requires the charger to provide "clean" dc power to the battery and prohibits the charger from introducing distortion to the ac input power.[4]

BATTERY CHARGER SYSTEMS

To determine the best battery charging system for the material handling application, several factors need to be considered. These include:

- Type of batteries used in the vehicle: automotive or traction, standard or maintenance-free, or fiber nickel cadmium.

- Battery rating.

- Total time the AGV is in operation per day.

- Type of AGV system: material delivery or assembly system.

- Breaks available for battery charging during the normal manufacturing operation.

- Availability to automatically charge or exchange batteries during normal operation.

- Variations in transportation requirements per AGV during a shift of operation.

- Peak transportation requirement periods.

- Auxiliary loads (lights, controls, heaters, etc.) that drain the battery continually whether under load, open-circuit, or on-charge.

Depending on the above factors, an AGV system will use one of the following four battery charging systems:

On-Board Manual Charge

AGVs operate for only one shift, then the batteries are recharged while the AGV is parked. This type of charging makes poor use of the vehicle and may require additional vehicles to support the system for an operation with two or more shifts.

The advantage with on-board manual charging is that it does not require a large battery exchange area, extra battery packs, and the support personnel for battery exchange. However it does require parking spaces for each vehicle during the charging cycle.

The disadvantage is that during the long battery charging cycles the vehicles are not available to do any work. Thus only the simplest and smallest of AGV systems use this type of battery charging.

Off-Board Manual Charge

This type of system is used for AGVs that run continually—operating 24 hours per day, 6 to 7 days per week. The battery packs are removed for charging; after they have been fully recharged to their recommended level, new battery packs are installed, and the AGV is put back into operation. The primary advantage of off-board manual charging is increased vehicle utilization; rather than having a vehicle

Figure 6.3 This is a battery charging and exchange station where batteries are removed from the vehicle, recharged batteries installed, and the discharged batteries recharged. A powered assist is used for the battery exchange. (Courtesy of Control Engineering Company, Harbor Springs, Michigan)

sitting idle during battery charging, the batteries are exchanged and the vehicle put back into service.

The disadvantages of off-board manual charging are the manpower required to change the batteries, the plant space required to store the spare batteries packs, the required battery chargers, and the preparation of the charging area to meet OSHA requirements. In AGV systems requiring many vehicles, off-board manual charging can be expensive.

The battery exchange should be made by one person in less than five minutes. Not all vehicles are designed to easily change the battery packs in a short time. Some vehicle manufacturers have a battery conveyor built into the vehicle to minimize the effort required to change battery packs.

Exchange of battery packs is the best way to increase vehicle use. The required utilization of the vehicle determines the number of spare battery packs required. Generally one battery pack is required per vehicle, per shift of operation. This will allow the batteries to be fully charged and properly cooled down before using; this provides maximum deep cycling, battery life and efficiency.

Figure 6.4 This photo shows the easy access to the battery compartments for exchanging batteries with a conventional pallet jack. (Courtesy of FMC Corporation, Material Handling Systems Division, Chalfont, Pennsylvania)

Automatic Charge

When the AGVs must operate 10 to 24 hours a day, a battery change at the end of a work shift is inconvenient and time-consuming. Thus, users frequently incorporate automatic battery charging into the system, linking the computer to the charger controls. When the AGV needs to be charged, or when vehicle transportation requirements are low, the vehicle automatically goes to the charging area. This type of charging system causes the batteries to be charged during production time, helps to better utilize the vehicle in a multiple-shift operation, and insures that more vehicles are available during peak periods. Automatic charging has made some AGV applications practical and cost-effective.

The vehicle must be equipped with a device for automatically connecting the vehicle to the battery recharging unit and the necessary control unit for automatic recharging. The vehicle drives into a charging station and automatically connects to a charger bracket, which is connected to the battery charger, and then the batteries begin to charge. Because of the frequent charging time the batteries are charged up to only 50-70% of capacity; this range keeps the optimum number of vehicles in operation. The custom-designed charging station is required, with a price approximately three times that of a manual connected charging station.

To optimize charging during production hours, it is necessary to know the future transportation requirements of the material handling system and when the peak requirements occur. If the system is controlled by specific production plans, proper vehicle planning can be achieved and the AGV batteries can be charged at pre-determined times. The advantage to this type of system should be clear—it would be inefficient if, immediately after vehicles are sent to the charging area, a high volume of transportation requirements needed to be handled by the system. This example illustrates the importance of anticipating production needs and establishing a production plan to achieve controlled battery charging and a higher utilization of the vehicles. It should be noted that the charging can occur before the AGV batteries are fully discharged and a low-battery condition exists.

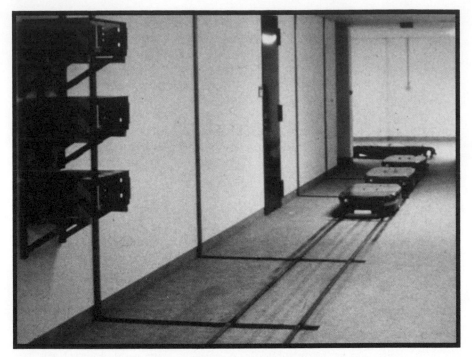

Figure 6.5 Three of TransLogic's Interchangeable Transcars are queued at automatic charging stations as they await their next transport command from the infrared communication box mounted in the ceiling. (Courtesy of TransLogic Corporation, Denver, Colorado)

With a good production plan and advanced charging, each AGV can be operated 14 to 16 hours per day.

Opportunity Charge

Opportunity charging is used when the vehicles have many short idle time periods and predictable stops can be defined on the vehicle guidepath. During this idle time the batteries are charged. These ideal time periods occur when one vehicle is waiting for another to move out of a station. The batteries are typically not discharged more than 10% to 30%. For example, in assembly systems where the AGVs are sequenced through the system, there are many short periods of waiting time when the batteries are charged. The short charge allows enough power for the vehicle to travel to the next work area. If this method of charging is selected, charging times must be carefully planned to make sure there are adequate opportunities for charging.

In most cases chargers are installed at all areas where the vehicles queue during idle periods, or at various points where assembly operations take place. Battery chargers are installed in the floor. At the bottom of the vehicle are contacts which connect to the charger when the vehicle stops over it. Thus, as the AGV waits, typically in a work cell or queue area, its batteries can be charged.

Opportunity charging was developed 1) to avoid taking vehicles out of service to charge the batteries, and eliminate the need for changing batteries daily, which is costly for large-scale systems; and 2) to provide a vehicle with a lower profile and reduced weight, due to the reduced battery capacity possible with frequent battery chargings. For these reasons most heavy capacity vehicles (over 20,000 pounds) use opportunity charging almost exclusively.

Opportunity charging has many advantages and can be best utilized in certain assembly and material handling systems; but it is mostly used in assembly systems. Opportunity charging reduces the cost of the total system by eliminating 1) floor space in the plant for charging the vehicles, 2) expensive ventilation systems in the battery charging areas, 3) special safety equipment, 4) specially treated floor, and 5) manpower—because no one is required to watch and maintain a charging area or supervise the charging of the vehicles.

The disadvantages to the opportunity charging system are: 1) explosive battery gases from battery charging are present in the work area if precautionary measures are not taken, 2) batteries are not returned to a fully-charged condition, which shortens battery life, 3) battery gassing creates an acid mist that settles on the AGV components, creating a maintenance problem, and 4) the type of batteries commonly used in opportunity charging have small capacities so their endurance is limited without charging. However, these disadvantages can be overcome by 1) Implementing a proper charging schedule, making sure batteries are not overcharged. In many cases batteries are charged to only 60% to 70% of full capacity during normal opportunity charging cycle. The batteries should periodically be restored to full charge at least every 30 days to prevent a gradual decline in capacity. 2) Equipping the vehicle with an exhaust fan that vents the battery compartments during the charging operation. 3) Using sealed maintenance-free batteries.

A typical opportunity charging application using sealed lead acid batteries, with a discharge load of 16.7 amp-hours per cycle, and a charging time of 40 minutes per cycle is shown in Table 6.3

TABLE 6.3 OPPORTUNITY CHARGING APPLICATION

Cycles	Battery Capacity Amp-Hrs	State of Charge %	Charging Amps	Amp-Hrs Retained	Battery Capacity Amp-Hrs
0	405.0	100			
1	388.3	96	8.1	4.12	392.5
2	375.8	93	8.1	4.28	380.1
3	363.4	90	8.1	4.43	367.9
4	351.2	87	8.1	4.58	355.8
5	399.1	84	8.1	4.74	343.9
6	327.2	81	8.1	4.89	332.1
7	315.4	78	15.1	9.41	324.8
8	308.2	76	24.0	15.19	323.4
9	306.7	76	25.8	16.39	323.1
10	306.4	76	26.2	16.62	323.1
11	306.4	76	26.2	16.62	323.1

In table 6.3 the steady state condition is obtained after the eighth cycle.

Lead acid batteries have been used extensively, in the US, with opportunity charging. Vehicles using lead acid batteries require long charging times over many short intervals; thus the vehicles are underutilized. But fiber nickel cadmium batteries are charged in a very short period of time. In fact, these batteries offer the flexibility to choose the specific battery size and recharge current to recharge the battery in the time available. The result is much better utilization of the vehicles.

BATTERY CHARGING AREA[5]

Two basic requirements should be emphasized when designing a charging area:

- What are the equipment requirements?
- What are the safety requirements?

For equipment requirements, it is necessary to determine the size or projected size of the vehicle fleet, shifts of operation, and locations. The issues that should be considered include:

- Number of AGV positions at each charger.
- Number of shifts the AGVs will operate.
- The position of equipment to remove and replace batteries by carts, cranes, or roll-out/roll-in conveyors, if there is more than one shift. Space requirement is a function of the battery change technique for the vehicles and the battery quantity per vehicle. AGV manufacturers can provide details on space and power requirements in the battery area.
- Special treatment of floors to resist acid spills, with controlled floor drains.
- Utilities required for cleaning the area and battery maintenance.

For the safety aspects, the following must be provided:

- Proper ventilation to reduce hazardous gas buildup.
- Deluge shower and eye wash.
- No-smoking area marked.
- Safety clothing and eye protection.

In addition, skilled manpower is required to change and charge batteries, add water, and clean and test batteries for defects.

A final comment: There has been considerable information published on the safety consideration of battery charging areas. OSHA (Occupational Safety and Health Act of 1970, as amended) current standards should be reviewed including 1926.403 battery rooms and battery charging, 1910.176 material handling and storage, and 1910.178 powered industrial trucks.

BATTERY CONNECTORS[5]

There are numerous types of battery connectors. Care should be taken to make sure the battery charger and vehicles are equipped with the same type of connectors. It's especially important to assure that there is no sparking or gapping of any electrical circuits that may create a hazard in the charging area.

REFERENCES

1) Eugene P. Finger, Edward M. Marwell, Eugene A. Sands, *Curtis Battery Book One/Lead Acid Traction Batteries*, 1981, Curtis Instruments, Inc., Mt. Kisco, New York.

2) "Fiber Nickel Cadmium Batteries" is based in part on: Michael Dodge, "Effective Battery Utilization in Automatic Guided Vehicles," Proceeding AGVS 1989, Volume 3, p. 47-65, The Material Handling Institute, Charlotte, North Carolina.

3) FNC-T Technical Bulletin, Hoppecke Battery Systems, Inc., Butler, New Jersey.

4) D. Plow, "Battery Charger Technology for AGVS Applications," 1986, Hobart Brothers Co., Troy, Ohio.

5) William O'Connell, Raymond A. Kulwiec, Editor, "Lift Trucks," *Material Handling Handbook*, second edition, p. 232-233, 1985, John Wiley & Sons, New York, New York.

Figure 7.1 This personal computer is the vehicle management controller. It processes the work orders, and selects the best available vehicle for a given assignment. This personal computer is connected to the material handling computer (Vax 8250 mini-computer system). The material handling computer reports to a host computer (IBM 3370). The material handling system includes 26 vehicles traveling over 25,000 feet of guidepath, delivering and returning material from 450 pickup and delivery stations. (Courtesy of Litton Industrial Automation, Hebron, Kentucky)

7 CONTROL SYSTEMS

The increasing integration of AGV systems into manufacturing operations presents new challenges in the control system. Larger systems, increased numbers of pickup and delivery stations, and more complex AGV activities all influence the complexity of the control system and the size of the program memory.

The evolution of AGV control systems has played a significant role in bringing more sophistication and automation to the factory floor. The controls are the brains of the system because they tie all facets together: AGVs, robotics, conveyors, machine tools, and human beings. Without state-of-the-art control systems, the integration of essential automatic functions would be impossible.

Technology in system control, data transmission, and computer processing has progressed to such a degree that many levels of AGV system control are now available. Each AGV vendor has his own control philosophy, using different hardware and software; thus there are as many design choices as there are AGV vendors. Because there are so many choices it is important that the controls be thoroughly thought out, identifying the specific requirements of an application (interfacing, networking, communication, information processing, and future requirements), and selecting the best hardware and control system to suit these requirements. This has become a formidable and complex task. The key to success is knowing what system or combination of systems will achieve optimum results.

The design of the AGV control system involves the ability of an individual vehicle to perform its required tasks, the coordination of many vehicles in executing the system transportation requirements, and the monitoring of the material handling system. This is achieved by determining the correct levels of "intelligence" to be allocated to the different system controllers and vehicles.

COMPUTER HIERARCHY

The control system is handled through a hierarchy of computers—generally four control systems integrated to form the complete system control. These control systems have separate microprocessor modules with real-time status and tracking. Depending on the complexity of the system, these different controls are found either in the AGV microprocessor (on-board control), or in the system computer (off-board control). The hierarchy of computers consists of host computer, system management computer, traffic controller and on-board vehicle controller.

Host Computer

The host computer directs the functions in the material handling systems (AGV, ASRS, conveyors, robots, etc.), maintains inventories, schedules production, holds database records, generates management reports on system performance, and controls other functions within the plant. The host computer conveys the tasks needed to be performed by the material handling system and receives data on the throughput achieved. If a host computer is required, it is generally provided by the buyer.

System Management Controller

The system management controller (commonly referred to as the central controller) manages the fleet of AGVs in an optimal way by coordinating vehicle schedules, making assignments for pickup and delivery of loads, and keeping updated on all assignments. It holds unused vehicles in specific locations in the system, monitors the battery charging of the vehicles, monitors problems that occur in the system, re-starts the system after it has been shut down, communicates with the host computer, compiles data for the host computer, performs supervisory functions for the AGV system, and can maintain inventory on the material in the

Figure 7.2 This is the central control system for a 19-vehicle system with over 11,000 feet of guidepath, and 31 drop-off and pickup points, for the Santa Rita jail. The central computer has a "hot" backup computer so if the first computer system malfunctions, the second can resume control. In the event of total loss of computer control, on-board vehicle control would allow the AGV system to continue functioning; this dual level of control further insures system uptime. Each central computer is a Compaq 286 with 640 KB RAM, and a 40 MB hard disk. (Courtesy of Apogee Robotics, Fort Collins, Colorado)

material handling system. AGV system management can be handled by a standard disk-based computer, which is easily upgraded as the system requirements grow, or by a personal computer, depending on the AGV system size.

One of the major advances in system controls is that more AGV vendors are controlling small to medium-size systems (10 to 20 vehicles) with personal computers. It is projected that by the early 1990s, systems of more than 50 vehicles will be controlled by personal computer. The expandability of the system is limited by the computer's capacity.

Figure 7.3 This AGV system operation console is located on the shop floor and provides the central control for a 30-vehicle system. The console provides an AGV tracking display, AGV system operations error display, AGV system activity monitor display, and an AGV task input terminal. This control system is driven by a Vax mini-computer system. (Courtesy of Mannesmann Demag, Grand Rapids, Michigan)

Traffic Controller

Scheduling several AGVs in a non-conflicting manner is a complicated real-time problem. As several vehicles perform their assignments in the system, new vehicles must be assigned tasks and put into the system without interfering with those vehicles. This is the job of the traffic controller, which coordinates all traffic to make sure there are no vehicle collisions and the AGV traffic is efficiently managed. If there are any problems with traffic, the traffic controller reroutes the vehicles and establishes new priorities.

The traffic control is a matrix control and can be handled in the same microprocessor as the system management controller, or in a separate processor. This controller holds all the information concerning the path network, routes, and timetable of all AGVs in process. Some traffic controllers will coordinate the anti-collision blocking controls.

When the traffic controller receives a transportation assignment, it selects a route and timetable that will not interfere with other vehicles and transmits this route to the assigned vehicle as a list of zone coordinates. The vehicle continuously reports its position and compares it with the positions required to reach its destination. Throughout the journey the vehicle monitors its expected arrival time at each zone and its speed to arrive on time.

The traffic controller calculates the time a vehicle spends in each guidepath zone on its route and compares the assignment with all other vehicles to determine if a new assignment conflicts with any current assignments. This is done for all vehicles with assignments. Tracking the time an AGV travels between two points is important in monitoring the vehicle, insuring that the shortest routes are used, and avoiding routes that may result in conflicts. If delays occur, new vehicles can avoid zones where vehicles are expected to be delayed. Lists are coordinated for all the vehicles to assist in controlling traffic and minimizing conflicts.

Some vendors use a traffic controller that passes the assignment to the vehicle, then lets the vehicle determine the best route to the destination. This has some advantages, such as lower costs, but overall the centralized traffic controller provides the most efficient schedule. In the final analysis both methods work, and the choice depends on vendor preference.

On-Board Vehicle Controller

The on-board vehicle controller controls vehicle guidance, steering, speed, acceleration, stopping, routing decisions, safety monitoring, collision and traffic avoidance, interface with pickup and delivery stations, doors, alarms, etc., communications with the central computer, and interface with other material handling equipment such as conveyors, ASRS, and robotic work cells. The on-board control should reduce to a minimum the dependence of individual vehicles on the system controllers.

There are several levels of on-board vehicle controls. The two extremes that use a system management controller and a traffic controller are 1) an on-board control that requires detailed drive and navigation instruction from the system management controller to travel between two points, and 2) an on-board control that has complete navigation capability and can control the vehicle between two points without detailed instruction from the system management controller.

In the first case, an assignment is given to an AGV with instructions that describe how the AGV drives from the present destination to the next sub-destination. The instructions include a series of steps with different functions, e.g., change steering frequency, change speed, change direction, etc.

In the second case, an assignment is given to an AGV with instructions that identify the AGV destination. The on-board software can navigate the vehicle from one destination to the next, and the AGV can drive (which frequency to follow, speed, etc.). The on-board software stores the guidepath segments in blocks of information containing the parameters of distances, vehicle direction, and vehicle speed. The path the vehicle travels consists of multiple routines strung together.

In both cases, at the final destination, the AGV gets a new assignment or stops and waits for the next instruction.

CONTROL PHILOSOPHY[1]

The sophistication of controls on-board the vehicle and within the AGV system depend on the control philosophy of the vendor. Most vendors follow one of two philosophies: centralized control and decentralized control.

Centralized and decentralized control systems can be broken down into three primary functions—system management, traffic control, and vehicle control—included in either the off-board or on-board controller. How these functions are integrated determines whether the control system is centralized or decentralized. Both control systems require intelligent vehicles, i.e., vehicles equipped with on-board microcomputers.

Centralized Control

The centralized control system incorporates the system management controller and traffic controller in one central location to handle the complete system. These two functions can use separate computers or be included in the same central computer, depending on the size of the AGV system. Figure 7.4 illustrates the block diagram for a centralized control system, and Tables 7.1 and 7.2 define the functions of the on-board and off-board controllers.

The system management controller includes the equipment required to communicate with the AGVs. This is commonly done by radio, infrared light, inductive communications through the guidewire, etc. The trend in industry is to use radio communication; therefore, radio is used in the following explanation.

The host computer creates the AGV tasks (material handling requirements) and passes them to the system management controller. The system management controller assigns AGVs a task or holding position (for idle AGVs), handles automatic battery charging, provides for AGV communication, and is the central location for receiving

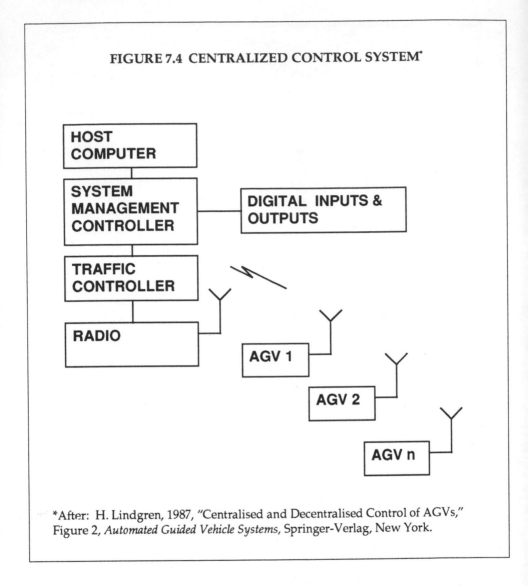

FIGURE 7.4 CENTRALIZED CONTROL SYSTEM*

*After: H. Lindgren, 1987, "Centralised and Decentralised Control of AGVs,"
Figure 2, *Automated Guided Vehicle Systems*, Springer-Verlag, New York.

communication from other equipment within the material
handling system (conveyors, sensors, P&D, etc.), that tells
when loads are waiting to be picked up.

The traffic controller gives routing instructions to the
AGVs. It has a description of the complete AGV guidepath
layout and tracks the current position of each AGV. The
common ways that an AGV records its position are de-

**TABLE 7.1 CENTRALIZED CONTROL SYSTEM
OFF-BOARD CONTROLLER FUNCTIONS**

Route Selection

Blocking Control

Load Scheduling

Empty Vehicle Distribution

Workstation Operations - Push Button/CRT

Optimum Assignment of Empty and Loaded Vehicles

Vehicle Tracking/Position Detection/Load Status on the
Vehicle

Inventory in the Material Handling System

Layout Description

Other Supervisory Functions

scribed in "System Reference Points" at the end of this
chapter.
 Advantages The primary advantages of a central system
 include:

- Centralized control systems provide real-time
  monitoring of all vehicles and activity within the
  system, primarily because they use continuous
  communication to monitor AGV status at all times.

- Installation is less expensive because the cost of floor
  cutting and wiring is reduced. This again is primarily

**TABLE 7.2 CENTRALIZED CONTROL SYSTEM
ON-BOARD CONTROLLER FUNCTIONS**

Communication link via one of the following:
- Radio to main computer
- Inductive communication through floor code plates
- Optical communication through stationary sensor and indicators

Controls guidepath monitor. If the vehicle strays from the guidepath, the on-board control shuts off the vehicle.

Performs diagnostics for troubleshooting the vehicle.

Controls safety and warning devices:
- Emergency bumpers
- Sonar and optical detectors
- Emergency stop buttons
- Audio and visual warning devices

Controls all vehicle operations and movement
- Drives
- Loading and unloading functions
- Steering instructions
- Navigating from point to point

---

because of the communication media. Several forms of communication can be used instead of loops, so floor cutting is minimized; only guidepath cutting is required. In addition, sub-controllers and the associated wiring are not required in a centralized system.

- It is easy to expand a centralized control system. The only changes required are the extension of the guidepath and reprogramming of the guidepath map held in the traffic controller. These systems are easily upgraded because they use a single traffic control linked to the system management controller.

- Extremely complex guidepath layouts can be used with these systems.

Disadvantages The disadvantages of the centralized system include:

- As a result of the constant communication media, the number of vehicles used in the system is limited— based on the speed of communication between the vehicles and the control system. For example, a radio channel can communicate with only a limited number of AGVs, therefore multiple channels are commonly required. Very large systems do not commonly use a centralized system.

- The central computer needs to be large and powerful for a large AGV system in order to handle all the data. The complete guidepath layout also must be stored in the central computer, which requires a large computer to process the AGV status data. The computer must communicate with the AGV and update the traffic controller on the AGV status in a timely way.

- A centralized system usually has only a few fixed positions where an AGV can be put back into the system after servicing. At each of these positions, the operator needs to specify the location of the AGV through an on-board terminal.

Decentralized Control

The decentralized control system is built with the same three controls (system management controller, traffic controller, and on-board vehicle controller); however, they are integrated differently in the control system. The decentralized control system is composed of a system management controller and sub-controllers. The system management controller has the system management responsibility and coordinates the activity of the sub-controllers, which have the traffic management responsibility. Figure 7.5 shows the block diagram for a decentralized control system, and Tables 7.3 and 7.4 define the control functions of the on-

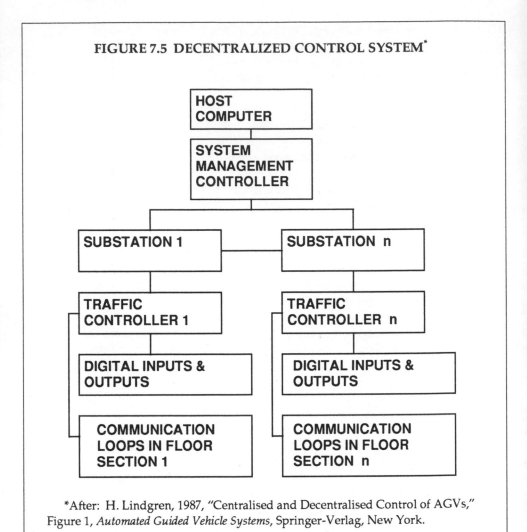

FIGURE 7.5 DECENTRALIZED CONTROL SYSTEM*

HOST COMPUTER

SYSTEM MANAGEMENT CONTROLLER

SUBSTATION 1

SUBSTATION n

TRAFFIC CONTROLLER 1

TRAFFIC CONTROLLER n

DIGITAL INPUTS & OUTPUTS

DIGITAL INPUTS & OUTPUTS

COMMUNICATION LOOPS IN FLOOR SECTION 1

COMMUNICATION LOOPS IN FLOOR SECTION n

*After: H. Lindgren, 1987, "Centralised and Decentralised Control of AGVs," Figure 1, *Automated Guided Vehicle Systems*, Springer-Verlag, New York.

board and off-board controller. With the decentralized control system both the system management controller and sub-controller are off-board.

The system management controller communicates with the substation controllers. There are typically several sub-controllers in the system. Each has a map of its segment of the guidepath and is responsible for controlling that segment. The sub-controller uses its map when giving direc-

TABLE 7.3 DECENTRALIZED CONTROL SYSTEM OFF-BOARD CONTROLLER FUNCTIONS

Route Selection (SUBSTATION CONTROLLER)

Blocking Control (SUBSTATION CONTROLLER)

Empty Vehicle Distribution (SUBSTATION CONTROLLER)

Workstation Operations - Push Button/CRT (SUBSTATION CONTROLLER)

Optimum Use of Empty and Loaded Vehicles (SUBSTATION CONTROLLER)

Vehicle Tracking/Position Detection/Status (SUBSTATION CONTROLLER)

Load Scheduling (SYSTEM MANAGEMENT CONTROL-LER)

Inventory (SYSTEM MANAGEMENT CONTROLLER)

Other Supervisory Functions (SYSTEM MANAGEMENT CONTROLLER)

tions to the vehicles. The sub-controller contains digital input and output interfaces, and communication interfaces to the system management controller and other sub-controllers and peripheral equipment.

Communication is via inductive communication loops in the floor, spaced along the guidepath and wired back to the individual sub-controllers. Because the loops are spaced along the guidepath, the vehicle is not in constant communication with the traffic controller. Information on AGV locations is not exact because the AGV reports only at each communication point, thus the traffic controller knows only that a vehicle is located somewhere between two communi-

```
┌─────────────────────────────────────────────────────┐
│                                                     │
│         TABLE 7.4  DECENTRALIZED CONTROL SYSTEM      │
│            ON-BOARD  CONTROLLER FUNCTIONS            │
│                                                     │
│  Communication medium-inductive communication       │
│                                                     │
│  Controls guidepath monitor.  If the vehicle strays │
│  from the guidepath, the on-board control shuts off │
│  the vehicle.                                       │
│                                                     │
│  Performs diagnostics for troubleshooting the       │
│  vehicle.                                           │
│                                                     │
│  Controls safety and warning devices:               │
│      • Emergency bumpers                             │
│      • Sonar and optical detectors                  │
│      • Emergency stop buttons                        │
│      • Audio and visual warning devices             │
│                                                     │
│  Controls all vehicle operations and movement       │
│      • Drives                                        │
│      • Loading and unloading functions              │
│      • Steering instructions                         │
│      • Navigating from point to point               │
│                                                     │
└─────────────────────────────────────────────────────┘
```

cation points. The AGV does not measure distances between communication points or detect anything to establish its current position. Generally, the on-board controller keeps track of the time the AGV travels between communication points. If the travel time between points exceeds the allotted time calculated by the computer, the computer shuts down the AGV and reports the problem to the system operator. Until the problem is corrected, that section of guidepath will be blocked and no traffic will be routed to that zone.

System decisions are made using the information from the host computer and current system information from the system management controller. The host computer creates the task and passes it to the system management controller, which decides what vehicle to assign to the task, then transfers the information to the sub-controller that controls the section of the guidepath where the AGV is operating.

The AGV is given the assignment by the sub-controller through the communication link. The vehicle's on-board microprocessor transmits the AGV status to the sub-controller, and the sub-controller tracks the AGV until it completes the task or leaves the guidepath segment controlled by that sub-controller. Information on the departing AGV is then sent from the sub-controller to the new sub-controller.

Advantages The primary advantages of the decentralized system include:

- It is easy to return an AGV to a decentralized system after servicing or repair. The AGV can be placed anywhere in the installation, because the central controller finds out directly where the AGV is located, through the sub-controller.

- Since each sub-controller controls a limited section of the AGV layout, it is possible to test each section during installation of the AGV system. This can be done before the entire layout is installed and before linking the sub-controllers to the system management controller. This enables the installation to be set up and tested in stages. As the stages are completed they can be put into operation if required.

  Furthermore, the many sub-controllers make it easier to expand the system because the entire system does not have to be redesigned. Either one sub-controller is redesigned or a sub-controller is added to the system. The system or parts of the system can still be operated as changes are made.

- The traffic control is completely handled at the sub-controller level, separate from the system management controller. Each sub-controller has its own map for traffic control. This feature allows the system to remain operational from a traffic standpoint even if the system management controller is shut down. After the system management controller has recovered, the full system can be put back into operation.

In addition, the many substation-controllers mean decision making is handled at a lower level, making the reaction or processing time much faster.

- A smaller central computer can be used in comparison to the centralized system because many of the system decisions are made at the sub-controllers. The central computer decides only the final destination of the AGV.

- A large number of vehicles can be controlled.

Disadvantages The disadvantages of a decentralized system include:

- Communication with the AGVs is through inductive loops in the floor. In large installations, there are many inductive loops, requiring extensive floor cutting to connect the loops to the substations. This additional wiring and floor cutting substantially increase the cost of the system.

- The decentralized system does not have real-time capability. The vehicle communicates with the sub-controller only at specific points; there are times when no communication to the vehicle can take place.

- Changing a decentralized system is more involved. The microprocessor will require changes, maps will need to be updated, guidepath re-laid, communication loop added and wired to the correct sub-controller. Any changes to the guidepath generally change the maps in several of the sub-controllers.

Summary

Figure 7.6 summarizes the most important advantages and disadvantages of decentralized and centralized systems. This figure indicates the generally accepted guideline of the listed attributes. For example, "troubleshooting" is clearly a positive advantage of the decentralized system because problems can be more easily traced to a specific substation;

FIGURE 7.6
SUMMARY OF THE IMPORTANT ADVANTAGES
AND DISADVANTAGES[*]

FUNCTION	DECENTRALIZED SYSTEM	CENTRALIZED SYSTEM
POSITION DETECTION	GENERAL IDEA OF VEHICLE LOCATION	PRECISE VEHICLE LOCATION
REAL-TIME MONITORING	NEGATIVE	POSITIVE
MAP	MANY MAP SEGMENTS	ONE CENTRAL MAP
INSTALLATION/START-UP	POSITIVE	NEGATIVE
P&D INTERFACE	NEUTRAL	NEUTRAL
TROUBLESHOOTING	POSITIVE	NEGATIVE
NUMBER OF AGVs SYSTEM CAN CONTROL	POSITIVE	NEGATIVE
FLOOR CUTTING	NEGATIVE	POSITIVE
COMMUNICATION WIRING	NEGATIVE	POSITIVE
COMMUNICATION TO AGV	NEGATIVE	POSITIVE
FUTURE EXPANSION	NEUTRAL	NEUTRAL

*After: H. Lindgren, 1987, "Centralised and Decentralised Control of AGVs," Table 2, *Automated Guided Vehicle Systems*, Springer-Verlag, New York.

in the centralized system, the problem must be solved by studying the entire system. "P&D interface" is not a clear advantage of one system over the other; however, in specific cases this may change, so the rating is neutral.

In selecting the AGV control system, factors such as materials flow and transport distances have to be considered. Generally a decentralized system is best in an installation with at least one of these characteristics: high materials flow, short transportation distances, many AGVs, and a complex AGV layout. A centralized control system is generally best when there is a large but simple AGV layout, high materials flow for long distances, fewer AGVs, real-time control required, and constantly changing material movement requirements.

SYSTEM ANTI-COLLISION BLOCKING CONTROLS[2]

Vehicle anti-collision controls are referred to as the blocking system. The blocking system directs traffic flow, maintaining a safe distance between vehicles, and prevents collisions at crossings, intersections, turns, junctions, doorways, and elevators.

The type of blocking system to be used is an important consideration. The anti-collision blocking design will influence system throughput, reliability, flexibility, and the ease with which systems may be modified or expanded. The wrong blocking system for a given application could limit a system's capability and efficiency, and increase operating costs.

Anti-collision blocking controls can be incorporated on-board the vehicle, along the guidepath, or in the traffic controller. There are two principal methods of anti-collision controls: zone blocking and forward sensing blocking. The choice depends on what the vendor has used in the past.

Zone Blocking

Most multiple-vehicle systems rely on some form of zone blocking, accomplished by three methods: point-to-point zone blocking, computer zone blocking, and continuous blocking. The selection depends on the size of the system, the sophistication of traffic control required, and the cost.

In a zone blocking system the guidepath is divided into segments or zones by switch elements and/or reference points. These reference points, located in the floor adjacent to the guidepath, define the zone. One zone is the distance between two reference points, sensors, or communication points. As the vehicle passes over a switch element, it checks in or out of a guidepath zone. The blocking control permits only one vehicle at a time to occupy a zone. While a vehicle is in a zone, that zone is reserved for that vehicle, and no other vehicle can enter. The status of the blocking zone is generally determined by the traffic controller or by the on-board vehicle control. The traffic controller monitors vehicle positions, and by constant reference to its blocking program determines which blocking zones are occupied.

When a vehicle occupies a zone it controls that zone, preventing oncoming vehicles from entering. The closest a trailing vehicle can get is into the next completely unoccupied zone behind the lead vehicle. Once the lead vehicle leaves the zone, the trailing vehicle can move ahead. A zone can contain one or several pickup and delivery stations. If a vehicle is allowed to occupy a zone, it can proceed to any P&D station in that zone.

In any form of zone blocking the number of zones depends on vehicle length and speed, system throughput, required safety distances between vehicles, and the number of turns, junctions and crossings within the system. In an efficient system with several vehicles, a zone length is typically the length of the vehicle plus 15 feet. While more zones increase the cost of the blocking system, they also increase vehicle movement within the system, speed, system flexibility, and throughput capability.

Point-to-Point Zone Blocking

Point-to-point zone blocking is a distributed zone control blocking using individual controls for each zone. The individual zone control boxes are mounted on building columns, walls, structure supports, overhead building trusses, special stands, or in the floor adjacent to each zone.

Communication between the vehicle and zone controller is usually via optical communication, using infrared sensors. These sensors can communicate with vehicles up to 10 feet away, allowing flexibility in the mounting of the sensors. They require a clear line of sight between the transmitter and receiver.

The sensor provides both the communication link between the traffic controller and the vehicle, and the blocking zone for traffic. When a vehicle passes an optical sensor it is recorded as leaving one zone and entering a new zone. The cleared zone is opened to be occupied by the proceeding vehicle. Until the vehicle reaches the next optical sensor, the traffic controller will not let another vehicle travel into that zone. As long as a vehicle has been permitted to enter a zone, it may continue to move and stop at any station within that zone.

Disadvantages of optical communication are that 1) moving obstacles in areas may interfere with the light source, 2) dirt on the sensors will interfere with the light source, 3) traffic controller is not in constant communication with the vehicle, 4) the system is more costly than computer zone blocking, but cost-efficient for small systems, and 5) it requires more maintenance than other blocking systems.

Another disadvantage is encountered when a vehicle is removed from the guidepath. To deactivate blocking, the vehicle that has been removed must be returned to the path exactly where it was removed and restarted to proceed into the next zone.

Point-to-point zone blocking is used predominantly in small- to medium-size systems (less than 3000 feet long, with four to five vehicles) where there are few zones. The more zones in the system, the more maintenance required and the higher the initial cost.

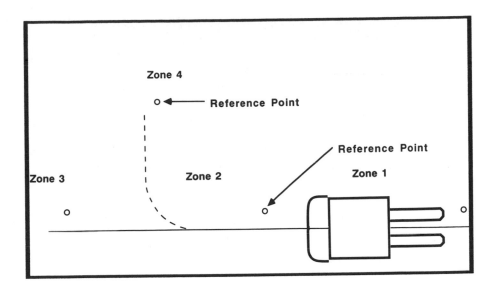

Figure 7.7 Guidepath zones are established by dividing the guidepath into segments. The zones are divided by switch elements and/or reference points.

Computer Zone Blocking

Computer zone blocking is achieved through the traffic controller that regulates the zones in the system. When a vehicle approaches a zone entrance, it communicates to the traffic controller, establishing its position and blocking status. The traffic controller determines if the vehicle can enter the zone. If the zone is clear the vehicle can continue; otherwise the vehicle stops and waits for instructions.

Computer zone blocking is used in systems that have several vehicles, and where traffic flow is constant. These systems are flexible and permit greater vehicle movement to achieve higher throughput. The disadvantage of computer zone blocking is that if the traffic controller is not operational, the entire AGV system cannot be operated.

Vehicles can be removed or inserted into the system at random without resetting blocked zones, and more complicated guidepath layouts can be installed and handled more efficiently. The biggest advantage of computer blocking is that it permits real-time vehicle tracking and monitoring, and vehicles with special assignment can have higher priority.

Blocking information may be communicated through the guidepath, FM radio link, separate data transmission wire, laser beam, etc. Methods of communication are discussed in further detail in a later chapter.

The vehicles carry an on-board microprocessor system that decodes blocking information picked up from the traffic controller. Each vehicle is equipped with a transmitting and receiving antenna. The vehicles communicate to other vehicles or a central computer controller either directly into the guidepath wire or through an FM radio link. When a central computer controller is used, it receives the zone information and keeps track of each vehicle location.

On-Board Control Blocking

This zone control blocking system is entirely controlled on-board the AGV and by all the AGVs in the system, with minimum assistance from the traffic controller. On-board control blocking requires an intelligent control system with sophisticated software. The vehicles determine their location by reading code plates in the floor, then transmit their location to all other vehicles in the immediate area. The vehicles use this information to decide whether they can proceed to the zone.

The advantages of this type of blocking control are 1) vehicles can be removed from the guidepath without resetting control boxes; 2) if a failure occurs in the blocking control only one vehicle is disabled, and the system can continue to operate; 3) the optimum number of zones can be installed for greatest possible vehicle movement and the lowest cost per zone.

Continuous Blocking

With continuous blocking, each vehicle has a transmitting and receiving antenna. When the vehicle drives over a special auxiliary continuous blocking wire, the vehicle transmits a high-frequency signal to the auxiliary wire buried in the floor, blocking other vehicles from passing over that wire.

Vehicle movement is stopped when the blocking loop generator feeds the loop a fixed blocking frequency. This frequency is recognized by a sensor coil on the vehicle that transmits signals to the vehicle's microprocessor to activate the brake. The vehicle remains blocked until the preceding vehicle with priority reports out of the blocking loop.

This system requires an extra wire embedded in the floor; its spacing depends on the system design. Continuous blocking is used primarily to control guidepath intersections, where vehicles are served first-come, first-served. There are no control units involved in continuous blocking, and practically no maintenance is required compared to a point-to-point blocking system.

This blocking method is not well-suited for systems where vehicles will be removed at random, unless system operation is strictly controlled. Usually continuous blocking is more expensive initially than point-to-point zone blocking because of floor cutting costs.

Forward Sensing Blocking Control

This control is incorporated in the vehicle by the use of sensors. It's found in all vehicles because of safety benefits, and in simple systems (system catalog 1) it also serves as the primary blocking control. The typical sensors used for forward sensing include sonar sensors, optical sensors, and mechanical bumpers.

Sensors are typically mounted on the front of the vehicle. As the vehicle moves forward, the sensor detects if the guidepath is open or if another vehicle (or object) is blocking the path. If the sensor detects a vehicle in the way of the advancing vehicle, the advancing vehicle proceeds in slow speed until its bumper hits the leading vehicle. The trailing vehicle then stops until the front vehicle advances; the trailing vehicle after a short delay then restarts and proceeds.

Forward sensing blocking is not foolproof. It's generally used in systems with a lot of straight paths and few curves. Because the vehicle's forward sensing controls detect straight ahead, they are not effective around curves, where they sense the area outside the guidepath. Continuous blocking loops can be installed on curves to enhance the forward sensing blocking system.

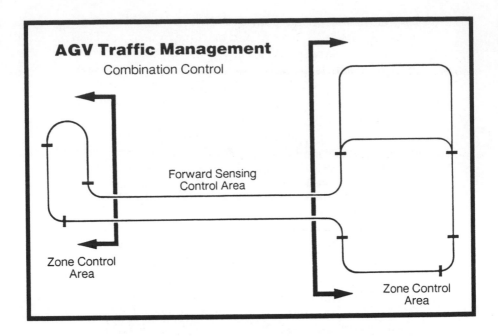

Figure 7.8 Combined blocking control system using zone control blocking on the curved section of the guidepath and forward sensing control for the straight section of the guidepath. (Courtesy of Gary Koff, Mannesmann Demag, Grand Rapids, Michigan)

Advantages of forward sensing blocking include: 1) It does not require fixed-length block zones, so vehicles can operate in close proximity for a greater density of vehicles in any given area. 2) Vehicles can be removed from or inserted onto the guidepath anywhere in the system without affecting the flow of other vehicles. 3) In systems with long straightaways, these controls reduce the overall cost of the blocking controls.

Usually AGV systems use one type of blocking system, but they can be designed with more than one method of blocking. In simple systems, for example, forward sensing blocking can be used on the straight paths and continuous blocking can be used on the curves. This improves safety and significantly reduces the cost of the traffic management system. But this combined control system provides no way to anticipate traffic flow and congestion, which could make a complicated system inefficient; therefore this blocking system is limited to simple systems.

System Reference Points

Reference points are an important part of the guidepath system. They may be used for various purposes: with the vehicle blocking system to establish zone boundaries; in vehicle navigation to identify where the vehicle is on the guidepath; and as decision points where the vehicle must communicate with the central computer before proceeding, or perform functions such as changing speed or sounding the horn.

In between reference points, some AGVs can measure distances and/or keep track of time, and report these intermediate positions to the computer. If the distances or time reported are not accurate (too much time or too great a distance), the computer shuts down the AGV and reports the problem to the system operator. Until the problem is corrected, the guidepath section where the inoperable AGV is believed to be is blocked, and no traffic is routed to that zone.

There are three common types of system reference points: incremental control, digital absolute control, and inductive data communication loops. These methods are often combined.

Incremental Control

For incremental control system reference points, cross wires, magnets, metal plates, or reflectors are installed in the ground or mounted at a fixed distance from the guidepath. These static elements help vehicles navigate through the system. The vehicle logic for navigation may be, "From intersection A count 5 magnets and deposit the load." As the vehicle travels the guidepath, it searches for and counts static elements using a software "pointer." Each time the vehicle encounters a reference point, its microprocessor moves the pointer to the appropriate position on the route map. The count of these references is audited after a specific number by a digital absolute element to ensure accuracy.

The disadvantage of the incremental control is that if the vehicle loses count of the static references, it is uncertain of its location until it arrives at a digital absolute element, or an operator corrects the problem.

Digital Absolute Control

Digital absolute control is critical to system operation, providing useful information to the vehicle. In this control system, each reference point is assigned an encoded address. When the vehicle encounters an absolute reference point it knows its exact location on the guidepath. The vehicle logic for navigation may be, "From reference point 35 go to reference point 56 and pick up a load." The vehicle doesn't need to count reference points to determine its position, thus eliminating any counting problems.

Digital absolute points are usually passive code devices such as metal plates, transponder devices, or radio frequency identification (RF) tags, cemented in holes drilled in the floor. Transponders and RF tags consist of an antenna plus a microchip. When the unit is energized by a specific frequency microwave beam, the tag transmits the data it holds. Some of these devices can be reprogrammed to modify the stored information.

These devices are located in the floor along the guidepath and used as location addresses or to initiate actions such as reducing speed for travel around curves and down ramps, activating vehicle horns, etc. As the AGV passes these devices it reads them to determine its location and block the distance between devices, preventing other AGVs from entering the zone it occupies.

The disadvantage of a digital absolute system is the software expense of programing these points into the route map. In large system layouts, it is not uncommon to have several hundred digital reference points.

Passive guidepaths often use bar codes located along the guidepath tape or the floor. These bar codes can indicate such things as stops, turns, intersections, restricted speed areas, location addresses, etc.

Inductive Data Communication Loops

Inductive data communication loops are fixed frequency loops, embedded in the floor at discrete points adjacent to the guidepath; a medium range frequency is used for these transmissions. The vehicle has a transmitter and receiver that facilitates direct communication between it and the controller. These loops may also use a constant coded serial data signal to transmit special commands to the vehicle or to send information about sections of the guidepath, e.g. reduce speed around curves or down ramps, sound vehicle horns, or activate equipment mounted on the vehicle. Communication is bi-directional and can occur with the vehicle traveling or stationary.

Figure 7.10 shows how these control devices can be used. As the vehicle travels it passes over one or more code plates or transponders in the floor. These code plates give location information to the vehicle so it knows where it is in the system layout. As the vehicle approaches its destination, it passes over a code plate. If only a single station is in the area, the vehicle uses the code plate as station recognition. If there are multiple stations near the vehicle destination, it looks for a station recognition magnet. This is all pre-programmed into the vehicle's on-board controller.

Passing the station recognition magnet activates a photoelectric sensor on-board the vehicle. When the sensor receives its reflection from a reflector, located on the station, it initiates a stop. When the stop is completed, the vehicle communicates to the station via infrared devices, one on-board the vehicle, the other on the station. This communication handshake coordinates load transfer by making sure the load stand is empty before the vehicle transfers a load, or that there is a load on the stand for the vehicle to pick up. Once the product is transferred the vehicle communicates to the AGV system controller through inductive data communication loop, in the floor. The AGV system controller then issues a new command to the vehicle.

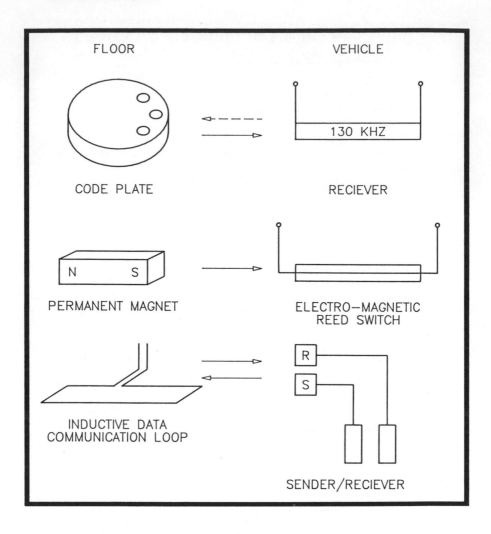

Figure 7.9 This illustration shows different system reference points that can be used in an AGV system. (Courtesy of Roberts Corporation, Lansing, Michigan)

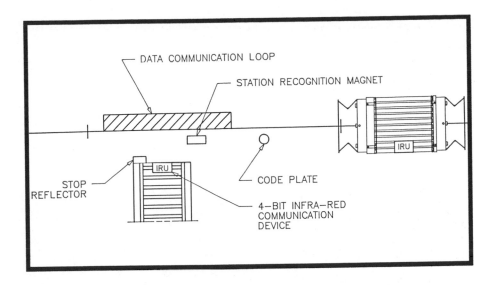

Figure 7.10 This illustration shows how a typical vehicle can be interfaced with a P&D station. (Courtesy of Roberts Corporation, Lansing, Michigan)

REFERENCES

1) "Control Philosophy" is based in part on: H. Lindgren, "Centralised and Decentralised Control of AGVs," *Automated Guided Vehicle Systems*, p. 79-86, 1987, Springer-Verlag, New York, New York.

2) "System Anti-Collision Blocking Controls" is based in part on: Gary A. Koff, R. A. Kulwiec, Editor, "Automated Guided Vehicles," *Material Handling Handbook*, second edition, p. 284-286, 1985, John Wiley & Sons, New York, New York.

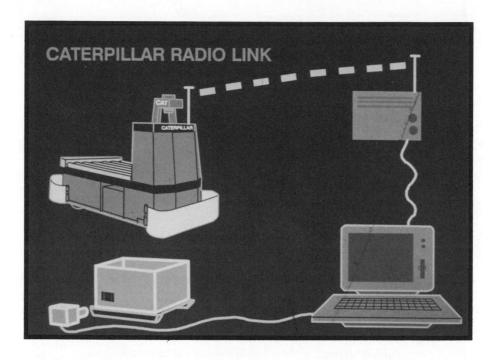

Figure 8.1 Landbase Computer Control System is the central information source for controlling the AGVs. Landbase Computer Control System assigns the appropriate vehicle and directs it to take the shortest available path. Vehicles and computer communicate by FM radio link. All call buttons, bar code readers, and load sensors are hardwired back to the computer. (Courtesy of Caterpillar Industrial, Mentor, Ohio)

8 AGV COMMUNICATIONS

Moving large amounts of data among the controller, vehicle, P&D stations, etc. requires planning to insure the proper exchange is made properly and efficiently. If too much time is required, the entire system may be too slow to handle the specified throughput.

Each communication application makes different demands for data transfer. The application determines the required data transfer rate, communication mode (simplex, half-duplex, full-duplex), whether two locations will be connected point to point, or a multiple-location network is required.

Data transmission rates fall in three specific ranges: low speed (bit rate up to 600 bits per second), medium speed (1200 to 2400 bits per second), and high speed (4800 bits per second and up). The maximum effective rate for a telephone line is 10,000 bits per second; most communication rates don't exceed 9600 bits per second. Most material handling applications will use medium speed data transmission.

After the data rate is established it is important to determine the mode of communication:

- Simplex is a simple system providing one-way communication with a transmitter at one point and a receiver at the other.

- Half-duplex provides two-way communication using a transmitter and receiver at each end. This type of system allows communication only one way at a time.

- Full-duplex provides two-way communication where two points can send and receive data simultaneously.

The type of communication, point-to-point or network, depends on whether the communication is between two stationary points or between many points whose number and location may change. An example of point-to-point is sensors on a pickup and delivery stand that are hard-wired back to a stationary controller. An example of a network is a continuous inductive communication system that communicates with several independent vehicles located throughout the entire system.

The main communication link in an AGV material handling system is between the AGV system controller and the vehicles. Data must be transferred from the system controller to the vehicle for remote automatic addressing of the vehicle, and for traffic control. This is accomplished through radio frequency transmission, limited distance infrared light, or inductive communication through the guidewire system or other wires. Each medium must be evaluated to determine the best one for the material handling system being installed.

Each medium uses a different response time, which will affect the operational efficiency of the system. The higher the efficiency (AGV system) required, the faster the communication should take place. Note that communication can be made while the vehicle is traveling or while it is stopped. In systems requiring real-time control, communication with the vehicle should be possible any time, regardless of its location, and while it is traveling.

The two general types of communication systems are local communication systems and central communication systems. Local systems transfer information when the vehicle is at a specific communication point; these typically use infrared light communication, and discrete inductive communication. Central systems use a continuous medium to transfer information any time, regardless of vehicle location, thus providing real-time control; these are typically radio and continuous inductive communication. The two systems have different applications.

Radio Communication

Radio has been one of the most popular ways to communicate with the vehicle and AGV system controller. When it was first introduced there were problems, but they have been solved.

Radio communication must be closely evaluated to be sure it will function properly. Success depends on the size of the computer, the number of vehicles, system layout, distance between P&D stations, the density of P&D stations, vehicle activity, peripheral equipment in the plant, and other frequencies transmitted throughout the plant and surrounding area.

A special consideration in using radio communication is the environment in which the vehicle operates. For example, cold storage applications can require special consideration with the antennas. Electromagnetic interference (EMI) with the radio equipment can also present problems. EMI is radio frequency noise that can be radiated or conducted and can affect the performance of electronic equipment. Sources of interference include welding machines, large motors, electrical equipment requiring much power, battery chargers, and some paging systems.

The location of the radio is critical. If radios are not properly located, the system will have dead zones—places where the vehicle cannot communicate with the AGV system controller. Dead zones occur because 1) noise is generated by surrounding equipment, 2) equipment on the floor can physically block the radio signal, and 3) the distance between the vehicle and the transmitter is too great.

In a material handling system where the transportation requirements have no set pattern, and 2 to 60 vehicles are operating, radio communication offers an advantage because the vehicle and the main computer are in continuous communication with each other. Vehicles don't have to be positioned over a particular communication loop to communicate with the main AGV system controller, or be located in line with special stationary equipment to be able to carry out its communication. Radio communication provides the greatest flexibility for changing vehicle destination routes. In an emergency, the destination can even be changed while the vehicle is en route.

Another advantage of radio communication is that it does not need to use any guidepath technology to function. If the AGV system requires dead reckoning navigation, the vehicle and AGV system controller can still maintain contact.

The AGV system controller, through the radio, rapidly polls the vehicles in a certain order approximately every second to determine vehicle identity, position, and status. Each vehicle answers back immediately, whether it is stationary or traveling. The AGV controller coordinates the data from all external sources (AGVs, sensors, P&D stands, etc.), and based on the system routing rules, instructs each vehicle: stop, start, new destination, etc., providing real-time control.

Different radio frequencies are used for different vehicles or different zones to provide more channel capacity. One radio frequency can communicate with and control only a finite number of vehicles at a time; therefore some systems will require more multiple radio channels to increase the effectiveness of communication and control a large number of AGVs. The radio transmission rate is between 1200 baud and 2400 baud.

The number of vehicles a radio can control depends on how the AGV vendor establishes the protocol between the AGV system controller and the vehicles. Some vendors allow communication to the vehicle only when it is necessary, eliminating unnecessary communication and hence

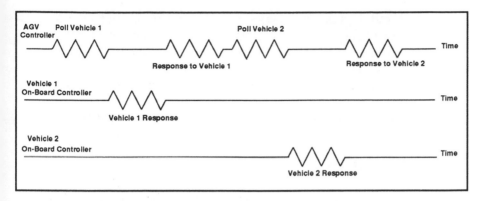

Figure 8.2 Vehicle polling is achieved through the communication media to determine vehicle identity, position, and status. The traffic controller is communicating constantly with the vehicles and only the vehicle addressed will respond to the communicated instructions.

wasted time. Other manufacturers continuously poll the vehicles but require only limited status updates most of the time, with occasional full status updates. Another procedure is to limit the number of communications to each vehicle. When communication occurs, it is a series of instructions which the vehicle stores and executes without further assistance from the AGV computer control. The benefit of these abbreviated communications is that more vehicles can be controlled on a single radio channel. Vendors are now controlling 30 vehicles on one channel.

The number of vehicles that can be communicated with also depends on the system layout. If vehicles are spaced throughout the system, the frequency of communication is reduced and more vehicles can be operated on one channel.

One of the disadvantages of radio communication is the procedure to obtain permits to use the required frequencies in the plant. Radio communications require an FCC (Federal Communications Commission) license. A permit for each frequency must be obtained, and the process can take three to six months. The user must know the exact location of the building (latitude and longitude), and conduct a radio frequency survey. The more frequencies required, the more difficulty in obtaining the permits. A frequency recommendation from Manufacturers' Radio Frequency Advisory Committee will speed up the FCC process.

Other disadvantages are: 1) radio communication can travel over a limited distance, and 2) radio equipment can be more expensive than other communication media. The equipment, radio transmitter and radio receiver, needed in each vehicle can increase vehicle cost by approximately 10%.

Infrared Light Communication

Another communication alternative is the use of infrared light. This medium is best suited for small systems operating in a clean environment. Because of the cleanness required, infrared light communications are generally not used for dirty industrial applications.

These systems are primarily point-to-point communications, where the vehicles must travel to specific points in the system to communicate with the AGV controller. There are two types of infrared relays (infrared transmitter and receiver unit) used in most systems.

The first type of communication method is through individual communication points located in discrete zones. Infrared relays are placed along the guidepath, attached to the building columns or mounted on the ceiling. As a vehicle passes a communication relay point, two-way communication can take place. Each relay can emit in the shape of a 15-degree cone. Therefore the relay on the vehicle must be aligned within 15 degrees of the stationary relay.

The second type of relay can communicate in a much larger window of space—an area of 350 square meters. These relays require the vehicle to be within this area for two-way communication between the vehicle and AGV controller. Because these devices cover large areas, there are only a few relays located in a system. In large guidepath layouts, each relay covers a section of guidepath, establishing communication islands. In an application where the communication islands overlap, continuous two-way communication with the vehicle and AGV system controller can occur. This type of communication has been used successfully in Europe.

The advantages of infrared are that it is fast, with a transmission rate of 19,200 bits per second, and it does not need to use any guidepath technology to function correctly. If the AGV system requires dead reckoning navigation, the vehicle and system controller can still maintain contact. Furthermore, infrared communication has two advantages over radio: lower cost for smaller systems and no licensing requirements.

Regardless of the type of communication system used, infrared technology will generally be used somewhere in the system. Infrared technology is best for communicating at fixed points where there is a clear line of sight between the receiver and emitter—for example, at a load transfer station for vehicle alignment, or between the host computer and AGV control system. This is a fast and effective medium for communicating and positioning the vehicle at the P&D stations.

INDUCTIVE COMMUNICATION

Because wire guidance is most commonly used, it is convenient for communication between the AGV system controller and vehicle to take place over wires placed in the floor. Inductive communication sends information to the AGV through the guidewire or an additional communication wire in the floor. The microprocessor on-board the vehicle receives commands through the buried loops and initiates vehicle functions.

Inductive communication uses higher frequencies than the guidewire system; typically the frequency is between 40 KHz and 120 KHz. A primary advantage of inductive communication is that it can transmit data at 9600 baud, faster than radio communication.

There are two basic types of inductive communication systems, discrete communication and constant communication. Discrete communication directs communication to a specific point in the system, and only one specific vehicle receives the message. Constant communication contacts the vehicle on a regular basis and all vehicles receive the message, but only the vehicle to which the information is directed acts on the information.

Discrete Communication

Discrete communication uses a separate network of wires that are laid in the floor and hard-wired back to a sub-station controller. The sub-station control is described in the control section, Figure 7.5, as a decentralized control system. Each sub-station has several communication loops connected to it, and feeds data to each loop. These loops are located at critical decision points throughout the system, near workstations, P&D stations, or wherever a decision or information must be transferred to or from the vehicle. Data can be transferred back and forth to an antenna on the vehicle as it passes over the inductive communication loops. The wires for much of this network may be laid in some of the same slots used for the guidewire.

At all decision and information points, the wires are routed out of the guidepath groove and formed into a communication loop. The communication loops are made long enough so the vehicle can receive data while traveling. If short loops are used, the vehicle must stop to receive the data. These loops transfer data that instruct the vehicle to follow specific frequencies in the wire and perform specific functions.

Discrete systems are most commonly used in assembly systems, where vehicles perform their tasks in a set pattern; one operation always follows a previous operation.

The major advantage of discrete communication is that it can effectively handle large material handling systems with many vehicles, because traffic control is relatively simple. The disadvantages include: 1) the communication loops are independent of the guidepath and require additional floor cutting, which makes the system expensive; 2) vehicles run in only one direction on the guidepath; 3) system changes

Figure 8.3 Intersection control for TransLogic's Transcar system is accomplished through transmit and receive inductive loops. These are shown embedded in the floor. They can be surface mounted as well. Loops also provide signals for automatic doors to open and close. (Courtesy of TransLogic Corporation, Denver, Colorado)

are more complicated to make and more expensive; 4) the system is static in that communication and vehicle functions are performed in a predetermined pattern, with vehicles operating in a specific sequence; 5) the vehicle can be put on or taken off the wire only at certain locations; and 6) no real-time control can be obtained.

Constant Communication System

In a constant communication system, data from the AGV system controller is transmitted to a vehicle-mounted data receiver through a continuous communication wire. The communication wire and the guidepath wire can use the same groove in the floor. The floor controller can either send data over a separate wire or superimpose the data on the guidepath wire. If the communication data and guidance frequency are sent on the same guidepath wire, the vehicle can pick up both guidance data and communication data and sort them. The vehicle can broadcast a signal to the communication wire, which acts as an antenna, providing two-way communication. Data transfer between the vehicle and AGV system controller can occur any place along the guidewire.

This type of communication is often compared to radio communication, because a signal from the control system is transmitted to all AGVs; but only the vehicle to which the message is directed acts on the data communicated. The advantage of the constant communication system is that the signal is transmitted over a distance of less than five inches, so electrical interference from surrounding equipment is minimized and many of the problems associated with radio communication are avoided. Also, a special license to use different frequencies is not required as in radio communication.

Another advantage of the constant communication system is that the vehicles can run in both directions on the guidepath. This is important because the system can be a random order of material requests, and the AGV system controller can select the best vehicle for the task versus assigning vehicles in a predetermined order. Constant communication systems offer flexibility compared to radio communication systems.

Constant communication systems are much cheaper to install than discrete systems because the floor grooves are used for both the guidepath and the communication system, reducing the floor cutting required. It is important to recognize that the less floor cutting required, the fewer the problems that can occur. However, fewer AGVs can be run in a constant communication system than in a discrete system.

It would seem that constant communication is always preferable to discrete communication, but this is not so; constant communication is not always needed. For example, it would not be practical in a large assembly system. Vehicles generally move in a predetermined sequence, and monitoring a large number of idle vehicles waiting to move into position would not be effective. Furthermore, a small material handling system would also make poor use of continuous communication. In such a system, the movement requirements are not that great, and it is not necessary to maintain constant status of the vehicle. The bottom line on communication is to understand the material handling requirements, now and in the future, and make sure the system being purchased can handle these requirements and can be expanded.

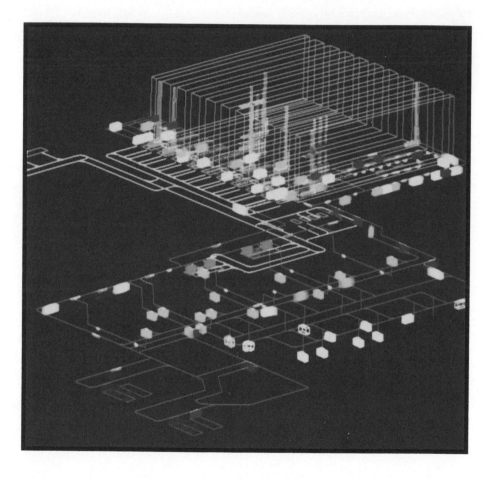

Figure 9.1 This is a simulation of an automated material handling system including an automated storage and retrieval system, automated guided vehicle system, and an automated electrified monorail system. The automated guided vehicle system moves material on the floor and the automated electrified monorail system moves material overhead. (Courtesy of Mannesmann Demag, Grand Rapids, Michigan)

9 SIZING THE AGV SYSTEM

This chapter discusses the fundamentals of sizing and developing the AGV system as well as estimating its price. The key fundamental is that the buyer must take an active role, to obtain a sense of confidence in what an AGV system can and can't do for him.

The buyer can let the vendor do all the work, but if the buyer doesn't get involved in system development, he is likely to have a finished system that he doesn't understand how to use—and he is likely to pay several hundred thousand dollars extra for the initial system design, system changes, training, and future maintenance. The buyer must understand and agree with the reasons for all aspects of the design. He'll obtain a better system and be able to negotiate a much better final price. The buyer can hire a third party to lead himself and the vendor, but he must still take an active part in design and implementation. The ultimate responsibility for the final system lies with the buyer!

An overview of AGV system development is shown in Figure 9.2: Flow Chart for Sizing the AGV System. This figure is broken down into two parts—buyer requirements and vendor requirements. The buyer should go through the identified steps to gain the information necessary to show the vendor the objective of the system. Also, the buyer will be in a much better position to evaluate the vendor's recommendation, make better decisions regarding the system, and eliminate any false starts.

The vendor and buyer cannot operate autonomously—they must work closely together. It is understandable that the buyer knows more about his product and processes than the vendor, and the vendor knows more about material handling systems than the buyer. The vendor draws upon the expertise of the buyer to understand the product, application, and buyer requirements. The buyer should have a broad understanding of the material handling technology being used. This exchange of technology and know-how must occur in the early phases of the project, before an order is ever signed.

The synergistic effort of buyer and vendor will produce the best system design and results. If the system is not designed properly, it may disrupt production rather than improve it. The buyer and vendor must have a close working relationship so they can openly discuss differences, alternative solutions, and the cost of each alternative. If potential vendors are not taking an intimate interest in the buyer's products or processes, the buyer should select a different vendor.

FIGURE 9.2: FLOW CHART FOR SIZING THE AGV SYSTEM

BUYER REQUIREMENTS

MATERIAL FLOW MATRIX

MATERIAL ACTIVITY LIST

PLAN OR REVIEW OF BUILDING LAYOUT

EVALUATION OF MATERIAL HANDLING ALTERNATIVES
- TOWLINES
- CONVEYORS
- SHUTTLE CARS
- FORKLIFT VEHICLES
- OVERHEAD CRANES
- AUTOMATED GUIDED VEHICLES
- ETC.

COST COMPARISON OF THE ALTERNATIVES

AGV GUIDEPATH ROUTING (IF AGVs ARE THE SELECTED ALTERNATIVE)

APPROXIMATE NUMBER OF VEHICLES REQUIRED (IF AGVs ARE THE SELECTED ALTERNATIVE)

AGV VENDOR REQUIREMENTS

DETAIL LAYOUT OF THE GUIDEPATH

EVALUATION OF SYSTEM ALTERNATIVES

MANUAL SYSTEM SIZING OR SIMULATION

VENDOR PROPOSAL

Determining the Number of AGVs Required

In sizing the AGV system, there are two ways to determine the number of AGVs required: a series of manual calculations and/or a computer simulation (which requires the aid of a computer and sophisticated software). The method used depends on the size of the system. However, for most systems it's best to do manual calculations for an initial estimate, to get an idea of the economics of using AGVs and determine if this is the correct approach. A personal computer can be used to assist with the manual calculations, to evaluate many alternatives and find the optimum system.

Manual calculations provide a first approximation for the number of vehicles required to operate the system, the number of P&D stations required, and the guidepath length. This evaluation is static; it evaluates one point in time with the assumption that the system is under steady state conditions and is not changing. To keep these calculations from becoming too complex, assumptions must be made for many factors such as speeds, load transfer times, variation in material flow, traffic conflicts, communications between vehicle and the system controller, etc.

However, the system requirements and resources are dynamic and constantly changing: number of pickup/delivery changes, number of AGVs available changes, traffic patterns change, status of P&D stands changes, etc. Therefore, manual calculations have limitations which can lead to uncertainty about the system parameters. As a result, the calculated system capacity will usually turn out to be either too large or too small.

The advantage of doing manual calculations is that it gives the buyer a broad understanding and appreciation of system requirements. The vendor will use these calculations in the initial sizing of the system as a basis for budget proposals. While the vendor may use a different calculation method, the principal ideas and assumptions will be essentially the same. When both the vendor and customer do the calculations, a synergistic result is obtained. In addition, the vendor will better understand what the buyer is trying to achieve, for better communication overall.

PROCEDURE FOR MANUAL CALCULATIONS

Material Flow and Movement

The most important step in evaluating the system design is the material flow analysis—determining from where to where the material is going. A material flow matrix gives an overview of the system even when no layout plan is available for the plant. The material flow matrix is a "from/to" chart, measuring the number of pickups and deliveries for each destination at both peak and average levels. It is difficult to determine average system activity, so several scenarios must be evaluated to get a representative plan. When the material flow matrix is complete, the throughput requirements for the system, for each department, and for each destination will be established. This information helps the designer of the system calculate the number of vehicles required to support system activity, identify the areas where capacity requirements are highest, and determine where system bottlenecks are most likely to occur.

The data from the material flow matrix is listed in order of highest ("from/to") activity. This helps the designer visualize the material flow and the intensity of the high activity areas within the system. The activity list can be expanded to show the distance an AGV must travel between pickup and delivery points, travel times, and number of AGVs required to support the throughput activities.

Even when the material flow matrix and activity list are complete an important piece of information is still missing:

Are any load accumulation areas (buffer storage) required? That information is necessary to determine if an intermediate buffer between the sources and destinations of the material flow will be required. There is a direct relationship between the flow of materials and the rate of productivity, and buffer storage is often the critical link to keep the material flowing. While "just in time" philosophy is demanding to minimize buffer storage, the efficiency and success of an AGV system depends on properly sized buffer storage.

Intermediate buffers may be required for non-transportation reasons. For example, if there is no available space in a work cell for the workpieces, they can be stored in the intermediate buffer. Buffers don't have to be located where floor space is at a premium; they can be at a remote location. Buffer requirements will be determined as each segment of the system is studied in greater detail.

Guidepath Routing

After all material movements to each location have been defined, the material movement is developed by determining the route of the guidepath in the building. The guidepath is designed to optimize system response time, one of the critical factors in determining system capacity. The more complex the guidepath, and thus the transport routes, the more planning of the guidepath is required. Other factors to be considered in planning the guidepath include the layout of the P&D stands, input loading points, the number of pallets that can be buffer-stored, buffer storage locations, vehicle parking, aisle width to handle either one-way or two-way AGV traffic, empty vehicle distribution, etc.

If the proposed material handling system is being installed in a new building, the vendor has more flexibility in making building changes to achieve a more efficient system and guidepath layout. In an existing building, changes will be minimized; hence, the flexibility to accommodate the material handling system will not be as great. It is important that the vendor understand what can or can't be changed in the building to accommodate the system and the guidepath layout.

The guidepath route is designed by comparing the material flow matrix and activity list with a plan view of the building. This building drawing should show the locations of fire doors, elevators, ramps, metal plates, manhole covers, fire hoses, drinking fountains, and pedestrian areas such as a lunch room, plant entrances, and exits. On the building drawing, locate the departments (from/to locations) and review the throughput of each department with the department's location in the plant.

It is best to determine the shortest possible guidepath route for the greatest vehicle activity in a descending order of vehicle activity. These distances may not actually be the shortest route, but the greatest vehicle activity should not be obstructed by lower activity tasks; thus alternate routes are required to reduce congestion. As each guidepath route is determined it should be marked on the building drawing, and the distance determined. These distances will be used to calculate the vehicle requirements for the system. Ideally, if the vehicle travels on the shortest route to its destination, the vehicle requirements will also be minimized.

In studying the guidepath layout, the shortest distance may not take the shortest time. For example, if a vehicle has to travel through an intersection where other vehicles must consistently travel, the vehicle may spend time in an idle mode waiting for other vehicles to clear the intersection. In these cases an alternate route may be faster even if the alternate route is longer.

Most areas should have multiple guidepath routes to each department to accommodate throughput requirements. If capacity requirements are high, there will be several routes; if capacity is low, there may be only one route. This planning step includes connecting the pickup and deposit stands with the guidepath.

Vehicles must be able to travel to all locations in the system and then return to their original location. Material flow requirements, P&D locations, vehicle traffic congestion, and empty vehicles distribution make it difficult to determine the best possible guidepath layout.

After the initial layout is complete, the designer should ask several questions about the location of each department:

- Do the locations of each department fit the overall plan?

- Are there any isolated departments where material flow will be restricted?

- Are heavy activity areas located too close together, causing congestion in the system?

- Have long dead-end spurs been avoided? Are buffer storage areas required?

- Are there enough alternate routes to areas of heavy activity?

- Is there room for AGV parking near all heavy activity areas?

- Could the design be expanded to support more activity, more AGV parking, and more AGVs?

- Will the vehicles be kept busy and not be required to travel empty?

- Have areas of heavy pedestrian traffic been avoided, and if not, are enough safety devices and warnings used?

- How could the system be expanded if production capacity changes?

Designing a guidepath route results in a system layout, AGV travel distances between departments, an approximate guidepath length and the number of guidepath elements. It is not critical that the exact distances between destinations be known at this time. From these approximated distances, each department's rough throughput can be determined. It must be remembered that the final guidepath will be determined by the vendor and ideally through a simulation study. This information is for an initial evaluation of the system alternatives.

System Spreadsheet

The next step is to make a spreadsheet on a personal computer, as shown in the example at the end of this chapter. This spreadsheet shows the material flow matrix, material activity list, AGV travel distances, AGV operating characteristics, and response time—all essential to understand the system throughput requirements and determine the number of vehicles required. The advantage of putting this information on computer is that any of the variables (material flow matrix, AGV speed, blocking time, deadhead time—defined later,—idle time, P&D time, and the number of AGVs) can be changed to evaluate a new alternative in finding the best system. By changing these variables, the designer will quickly understand which are important and how they affect throughput. Typical "what if" questions to ask are:

- If vehicles are down for maintenance, what happens to the throughput?

- If the speed of the AGV can be increased, what happens to the number of vehicles required in the system?

- If a department's throughput requirement increases, how many vehicles are required to support the demand?

- If P&D time increases, what happens to the vehicle requirements?

The assumptions made in selecting the proposed system must be noted so they can be verified at a later date.

System Simulation[1,2,3,4]

While manual system calculations provide an overview of system requirements, they don't enable the designer to determine the effects of 1) the average waiting time between moves, and the average distance a vehicle moves without a load; 2) the correct buffer capacities and location to keep the number of vehicles as low as possible; 3) the dynamics of the system evaluating vehicle movement, such as the load on the system elements, the average number of vehicles per hour passing through a guidepath crossing, etc.; 4) vehicle performance data such as speed variations, acceleration, and deceleration; and 5) control rules and right-of-way rules. As material handling systems get larger and more complex, these items make it more difficult to find the best system. They can be determined by a system simulation and should be worked out accurately before the system is installed; mistakes can be difficult to correct after installation.

If the buyer or vendor believes a simulation is required, it should be carried out before order placement and should be conducted by the potential vendor or by an independent organization, with the vendor taking full responsibility. While simulations save time and money in system planning and implementation, they are not cheap. Typical costs range from $30,000 to $70,000. The general rule of thumb is that for large systems the simulation analysis cost is 3% to 5% of the total project cost. Considerable time is also required to develop an accurate simulation model, from several weeks to a few months.

Simulation is used by only a fraction of the nation's industrial firms, although Fortune 500 companies generally require it before approving major capital projects. Many small and mid-size companies still consider simulation too exotic and expensive. Even experienced buyers are only now realizing the need to get these powerful tools out of the computer room and onto the shop floor.

Yet experience proves that a computer simulation is a necessary and economical tool in planning AGV systems. There are so many factors to consider, so many alternatives to be thought through, that the proper tools must be used for system design. A simulation study can be one of the most important keys to a successful automated material handling system.

Simulation of the proposed system by a computer model has two advantages:

- It will prove that the system being purchased will perform to the desired specification and is sized correctly, maximizing equipment use while minimizing inventory, work-in-process, and labor costs. Simulation permits study of the dynamics, random system demands, production changes due to human factors, distribution of empty AGVs, assignment of AGVs to specific tasks, and erratic traffic patterns; these models produce accurate results. If modifications to the system are required, they can be resolved before installation.

- It will be used to test the operation of the system and insure that it meets performance criteria: downtime, operation time, battery charging, effects of rework, queuing, capacity, availability, number of AGVs required, reliability, etc.

The tendency in putting together a system is to view it as individual events rather than correctly viewing it as a synergistic series of individual activities flowing simultaneously. Simulation allows material handling systems to be analyzed as systems and not merely as individual components. AGV systems can be modeled and experiments conducted to understand the behavior of the entire system before it is ever built, eliminating costly experimentation on the factory floor and minimizing the risk to a potential buyer. A simulation study is cheap insurance.

The following questions can help determine whether a simulation is required. A "yes" answer to any of them may justify doing a simulation:

- Is there a sequence of events where certain events must be completed before others start?

- Is there a guaranteed system throughput?

- Do any system components operate at utilization rates over 85%?

- Are there large variations in process times?

- Are there new algorithms for process control?

- Does the system require synchronization with other systems?

- Do any system activities in which timing is critical depend on people?

System Definition

To run a simulation, all system equipment (AGVs, AS/RS, conveyors, sizing stations, etc.) must be determined in advance and located in a layout. When preliminary equipment selection is complete the simulation models the entire material handling system. For AGVs alone, numerous variables must be considered to achieve a smoothly running system: the guidepath network, communication method, communication times, type and number of AGVs, AGV speeds, location of blocking points, speed zones, floor deposit locations, distribution of loads to deposit stations, transfer times at P&D stations, alternate AGV routes, load stand configuration, workstation configuration, conveyor and conveyor control information, and vehicle management protocol.

The model simulates AGVs moving from one destination to the next, delivering loads and performing tasks while interacting with the peripheral equipment and all other surrounding influences. At each destination, loads are deposited or picked up, and the next operation is completed for that load. Provisions are made in the simulation for idle load time in storage, machining time, or assembly labor. All functions of the system are performed the way they will be when the actual system is installed. In essence the simulation creates a time record of every event, and every vehicle action, and tracks every load.

System Analysis

The simulation requires considerable effort and numerous runs to investigate several alternatives and material handling philosophies. It will enable the designer to determine the ability of the factory to work on a just-in-time basis with small lot sizes and short lead times, and evaluate several system parameters to determine the optimum system design and the most cost-effective layout. The designer will make diagnostic analyses, make changes, simulate again and continue the process until the system shows the characteristics that the designer wants. The designer has to optimize the system step by step, and it is imperative that he understands what he is modeling.

One facet of material handling that can be properly evaluated by simulation is the need for buffer storage or distribution queues throughout the system. Buffer storage requirements are a function of vehicle response time, and keep the production process from starving for parts. Alternatives include[1] 1) high buffer storage capacity, low transportation capacity (small number of AGVs utilized extensively, resulting in long transportation times), or 2) high transportation capacity, low buffer storage capacity (large number of AGVs with a low utilization rate, resulting in short transportation times). Experience has proved that decisions on these compromises can be achieved only by use of detailed simulation studies. Before running a simulation, however, it is necessary to determine the degree of efficiency and utilization of the vehicles. This degree of efficiency determines the necessary buffer space.

To set up a system simulation, define mathematically the layout of the facility and the activity rates required at key points throughout the system. From this information the computer helps the designer determine a system layout. The simulation model copes with vehicle breakdowns, blockages, and departures from the intended journeys. It guards against unanticipated bottlenecks by reducing system inefficiencies (delay times, losses due to product and/or model mix) that can be created by having too many or too few pallets, load/unload stations, AGVs, and material feeders. For specific applications the simulation helps determine the best guidepath networks, the optimum number of vehicles, and the most efficient position for pickup and delivery stations or workstations. In a properly designed system, the simulation determines the final system layout.

Here is a summary of the objectives to be achieved using simulation[2]:

Provide the Plant Layout
• Optimum design of guidepath and intersection points.

Identify utilization of P&D stations and the guidepath around those P&D stations. Eliminate weak points, bottlenecks, and mistakes in the layout.

Provide a Manufacturing Model
- Identify workpiece types
- Determine system capacity
- Evaluate product mixing
- Obtain production balancing
- Plan for storage of the product

Provide a Manpower Planning Tool
- Determine number of support people needed
- Plan assignment of workers

Provide a Manufacturing Planning Tool
- Production capacity
- Work-in-process
- Loading of workstations
- Loading of buffer storage
- Size and placement of buffer storage
- Capacity reserves
- System bottlenecks
- Proper number of workstations
- Flow of information

Define the Transportation System
- Best vehicle routing
  - -Shortest routes and detours
- Vehicles
  - -quantity
  - - rate of utilization
  - - loaded and empty trips
  - - workpiece exchanges
  - - buffer times
- Buffer storage for work in process
  - -Locations of buffers
  - -Capacity of buffers
- Best vehicle management protocol
  - -First-in-first-out
  - -Vehicle closest to the load
  - -Dispatched loads look for the next available vehicle

Another benefit of simulation is that system hardware and software can be planned in detail, demonstrated, and checked for compatibility before installation. The AGV system controller uses the actual software developed to control the AGV network, scheduling individual vehicle task assignments, and operating in real time.

A simulation shows the buyer what happens to system output when any of the parameters change and permits evaluation of the automation alternatives. The system can be installed, checked out, and debugged in minimum time with no capital investment, giving the customer a low-cost way to consider all the variables. A simulation cuts installation time, and saves as much as six months to one year delay time. In short, simulation provides the buyer with the best chance that the new material handling system will perform as planned.

After the simulation these questions can be answered:

- What happens if the material flows are increased?

- Does the system require any sizing stations?

- How many AGVs does the system require?

- Where are the limiting bottlenecks in the system?

- How many AGVs have passed a certain point in the layout?

- Which routes should the AGVs use in traveling to each destination?

- What alternative routes have been considered?

- What is the AGV waiting time at a certain point in the layout?

- What is the utilization of a certain segment of guidepath?

- For how long is a certain segment of guidepath blocked?

- How many loads are picked up at a P&D station?

- How many loads are deposited in a P&D station?

- What are the number of loads in queues?

- What is the average time the AGV is loaded?

- What is the average time the AGV is empty?

- What is the average time the AGV is idle?

- What is the average waiting time for a pallet at a pickup position?

- What is the average time the AGV is in the battery charging area?

- What is the number of assignments performed by each AGV?

- What is the maximum system capacity (throughput)?

- What are the buffer requirements?

- Should the guidepath be bi-directional?

- Should the vehicles be bi-directional?

- When an AGV is required, how is it chosen?

- How should the tasks of AGVs be prioritized?

- How should the priorities at the guidepath intersections be considered?

Documentation Requirements

After the simulation is run, the vendor must decide how the results are to be shown—in a numerical report showing the statistical results and/or an animated presentation using computer graphics. Because manufacturing is dynamic, animation offers valuable advantages over statistical reports, which show only a snapshot of the process. The best way for the buyer to understand the system parameters and their effects on performance is to insist that the vendor use computer graphics to animate the simulation, displaying AGV movement directly on screen. This shows clearly how the final system works and aids in further system refinement. Furthermore, it provides the opportunity to recheck the system layout and observe its function, understand the dynamics of the system, and identify high traffic and problem areas.

Selecting the simulation language is important in determining what in the proposed system will be modeled, and how it will be modeled. The common languages used in material handling systems are:

- AutoMod/AutoGram, available through AutoSimulations, Incorporated.

- GPSS, available through Wolverine Software Corporation.

- SIMAN, available through Systems Modeling Corporation.

- SLAM II, available through Pritsker & Associates, Incorporated.

- TESS, available through Pritsker & Associates, Incorporated.

Extensive efforts on AGV system optimizing and selection justify using computer simulation to achieve a cost-effective system. As systems, and integrating those systems, become more complex, computer simulation takes on a more important role in planning a factory's material handling system.

Availability and Capacity[3]

Two of the most important terms in understanding the utilization of a system are *availability* and *capacity*. Availability is the percent of the total running time during which a system is functional. Capacity is the number of loads (throughput) that the system can handle at 100% availability. Generally system capacity decreases as a system's availability decreases.

System capacity and availability should be determined independently. When determining availability it is important only to make sure that the system can carry out its functions with no interruptions. In determining system capacity, it is important to evaluate at what availability 100% capacity is achieved.

To determine availability of the entire system, each single component must be evaluated to determine its availability; system components are either functioning or not. The type and location of a component determines if the system will become inoperable if the component fails. If the component part is in parallel, an individual component can fail and the system availability will be maintained. However, if the component is in series, a failure will shut the system down and make it unavailable.

Early in the design of the system, every component should be evaluated on two points: Is it in series or parallel with the entire system? And what is its impact on system availability or capacity? A detailed analysis of the effect of a breakdown of each component should be done. Then the system should be designed to minimize the effect of any breakdown. This helps produce high system availability and an efficient layout design.

Two examples illustrate system availability with a parallel component and a series component. First, the parallel components: If an AGV system has 20 vehicles and one of those vehicles breaks down, the system can continue to operate with the remaining 19 vehicles. System capacity has been reduced by 5%, while system availability remains 100%. However, it is also highly probable, if the requirements on the system are not too heavy, that the system will continue to operate at a capacity that satisfies the system requirements.

Second, the series components: If the central computer for the system becomes inoperable, the entire material handling transportation system will become inoperable. Provisions can be made for complete computer system backup or for manual intervention.

Availability should be further defined in terms of the maximum acceptable period of activity. For example, a one-shift operation has 21 shifts per month. If the system is not operational for one shift, system availability is 95.2%. On a two-shift operation the system availability would be 90.4%.

As the system ages, the frequency of repair increases as the system components wear out, which adds to the problem of system availability. In many cases, good preventive maintenance, an adequate stock of spare parts, backup AGVs, and backup computer equipment support the system to obtain the optimum availability. To increase system availability it is important to carefully think through and plan a preventive maintenance program. Diagnostic capability for system components is also important to minimize downtime. This can have a substantial impact on getting the equipment back into service, thus improving the availability of the system. With good service, and a well designed system, system availability can be 90-97%.

While higher availability is generally expensive to accomplish, there are two ways to do it. The first is to increase the reliability of every system component by providing redundancy (a backup component); most systems will have some redundancy built in. With redundancy, individual components can have a lower reliability, but the overall reliability of the system will be improved. In many cases, however, redundancy is used to improve components that are already better than required, thus wasting money. Redundancy can be expensive because of the many computer components that need backup. The second way to improve system availability is to supply an alternate way to transport material in the event of a failure. The overall capacity of the system is greatly reduced, but the product can still be moved.

Applications requiring high availability include automotive systems and newspaper material handling systems, which cost thousands of dollars per minute when the AGV system is not in operation. It is not difficult to justify complete backup for critical components in these systems.

The capacity of a system is generally measured in terms of unit loads per some time element at 100% availability. Actual capacity should be roughly 65% to 85% of rated capacity. This guideline helps eliminate capacity problems that may result if system availability falls by a few percent. The total capacity is affected by too many random variables to operate at a higher rated capacity. The capacity of a system is difficult to calculate or evaluate other than by simulation or by actual operation of the system.

In calculating availability, the availability of each component must be known as well as whether it is in series or in parallel with the rest of the system. For components running in series, the overall availability is the product of the uptime availability of each component: $N=(n_a)(n_b)$. For parallel components, the availability is calculated using this formula: $N=1-(1-n_a)(1-n_b)$; n_a=availability of component a, n_b=availability of component b, etc.

For example, consider a simple material delivery system using five AGVs, each with 90% availability; the traffic controller, with 95% availability; and an input and output conveyor with 99% availability. Here's how to determine the overall availability.

The five AGVs are in parallel with the system and their availability is:

$$N=1-(1-n_a)(1-n_b)(1-n_c)(1-n_d)(1-n_e)$$
$$N=1-(1-n_{agv})^5$$
$$N=1-(.90)^5$$
$$N= 99.99\%$$

The overall system is now in series and the availability is

% AGV	(.99)
% traffic controller	(.95)
% input conveyor	(.99)
% output conveyor	(.99)

$N=(n_a)(n_b)(n_c)(n_d)$
$N=(.99)(.95)(.99)(.99) = 92\%$, the overall availability of the system.

Limiting Factors

In designing or improving a system, it is important to review all aspects of the system, because each one may be the limiting factor restricting the system throughput. The following list of factors should be considered:

AGV Speed

The normal pressures of automation make higher speeds desirable. Increased speed influences transportation time and increases the utilization rate of all equipment in the system. Speed is important in achieving the maximum utilization of the vehicles, especially on long-distance runs. The rule of thumb is that a 25% increase in AGV speed will increase capacity (throughput) between 10-15%. At the end of this chapter is an example showing the effects of speed versus the number of AGVs required for a system.

The AGV's speed changes depending where the vehicle is on the guidepath. Typically on curves the vehicle slows to as much as 40% to 50% of the rated speed; to 20% to 30% of maximum speed while looking for sensed obstacles in the guidepath; and to 40%-60% of full rated speed traveling in reverse.

Maximum vehicle speed for straight paths depends on the type of vehicle. The typical range is from 90 to 300 feet per minute; the average speed of most vehicles is approximately 180 feet per minute. In estimating actual system throughput, allowances must be made for slower speeds due to turning, sensed obstacles, etc.

P&D Times

P&D load transfer time is important in increasing throughput capabilities. A reduction in P&D times influences system capacity more than AGV speed does. The transfer time influences the time the AGV waits for the material transfer to be made. At some point, increasing the number of AGVs will not produce a good return on investment because of the P&D time. In applications with short distances, it is important to make sure that vehicle utilization rates are kept below 50% to insure system throughput requirements are achieved.

Battery Charging Zones

Vehicles cannot run continuously; their batteries must be either charged or replaced. To have the majority of AGVs available during peak production times, vehicles should be charged throughout the day. It is important to coordinate battery charging with the day's production requirements to optimize charging and vehicle utilization. Battery charging areas are provided for this reason, generally in a remote location. Generally an AGV runs for one shift of operation before the batteries need servicing. See the battery charging chapter for different battery options.

Traffic Planning

Each intersection can contain only one AGV at a time. Thus several vehicles can be waiting to enter an intersection at any one time. High throughput areas in the system should have multiple routes to eliminate congestion at busy intersections.

When vehicles are not required, they must be parked and in a sleep mode. The queue location can be on or off the guidepath. An off-the-guidepath queue or spur could establish better flow in the network, allowing for passing vehicle traffic. Multiple queueing locations for unassigned vehicles can be incorporated in the guidepath design. To avoid traffic congestion, one parking place should be available for every vehicle in the system, and pickup and deposit stations should be adjacent to each other. This depends on the size of the guidepath network and the proximity of these queue points to the required pickup and drop-off locations. The guidepath should be laid out to allow easy access from queue locations to each dispatch location. It is a general rule to have ample parking adjacent to high activity areas.

Calculating Number of Vehicles Required

Now that the procedure for designing a system has been discussed, the definitions and formulas used in the manual calculations for a system design will be stated. Following these definitions is an example that shows sample calculations for several of the definitions.

System Capacity

The throughput rate at which the system operates is the system capacity. If the number of pickups and deliveries changes, the system capacity also changes. The material flow analysis is done for the nominal condition; if more activity is expected, the system capacity figure will change. The capacity of a material handling system can easily change during a shift of operation, due to part shortages or efforts to make up for lost production. Because of these changes in production requirements, it is best to consider several scenarios in the evaluation.

One way to handle these different scenarios is to use peak loading factors. Systems are generally designed to handle a specific throughput, but on occasion a system will exceed the design throughput; this is "peak loading." Peak loading can be evaluated by multiplying throughput by the peaking factor. Typical peak loading factors are 1.15 to 1.30 (15 to 30%) for distribution operations, 1.10 to 1.20 (10 to 20%) in manufacturing[5].

Throughput

Throughput is defined as one complete load pickup and deposit. This requirement can be for either a component of the system or for the complete system—e.g., throughput from inspection to final assembly or throughput for the complete system.

The rule of thumb is a vehicle can handle 5 to 10 loads per hour. This rule is based on these assumptions: 1) the average distance the vehicle travels for one pickup and delivery is 1400 feet, 2) the average speed a vehicle travels is 175 feet per minute, 3) the vehicle load and unload time is one minute, and 4) the vehicle will be parked or blocked in traffic for one minute. Using the above assumptions the exact throughput per vehicle would be six loads per hour.

Travel Distance (d)

The travel distance is the length of guidepath, in feet, which a vehicle covers between two points—e.g., the distance the vehicle must travel to get from inspection to final assembly. This is typically the shortest distance between the two points. While there are generally several alternate routes between two points in the system, the shortest distance is listed in the analysis. The shortest routes cannot always be taken, however, so this is accounted for in the deadhead time.

Deadhead Time $(t_d)^5$

This is the time, in minutes, vehicles travel without a load to pick up the next load or travel to a parking space after depositing a load. The deadhead time factor is K_d. This factor can be quite large because many things affect it, including the extra time the vehicle takes in using alternative routes, acceleration and deceleration of the vehicle, and the reduced speed of vehicles traveling around curves and in reverse. As the system requires more and more vehicles, traffic control becomes more complex and vehicles use alternative routes more consistently.

Another substantial influence on deadhead time is the dispatch method. A FIFO (first-in first-out) dispatch scheme, where tasks are assigned to vehicles in order of their availability, underutilizes the vehicle because it may deadhead unnecessarily long distances to secure new assignments. Strict FIFO dispatching can reduce system productivity by 20% to 30%. Instead as vehicles become available they should look for their next assignment near their present location, or be parked nearby in anticipation of an assignment, or be dispatched to an area where current empty vehicles are needed.

If the vehicle always travels with a load and has no deadheading, $K_d = O$ for travel. Moreover, if the vehicle deadheads the same distance it traveled to a P&D when it was loaded, $K_d = 1.0$. Excessive deadhead travel means K will exceed 1.0. Therefore, the lower the K_d factor the better. As a rule of thumb, the K_d factor should be 0.45 - 0.65 for small, highly optimized computer-controlled systems; 0.60 - 1.0 for larger optimized systems. It should be noted that it's difficult to determine accurate utilization factors for AGVs; factors have been guaranteed for only simple applications. The formula is: $t_d = K_d t_R$, where t_R is the run time.

Using the deadhead time, the actual distribution of empty vehicles is not considered, but this factor accounts for additional vehicle travel, thus accounting for the distribution of empty vehicles. A more complex manual method to account for empty vehicle distribution is presented in reference 6.

In reference 6 several approaches to handle empty vehicle distributions are discussed. In essence the proposed procedure is to define the guidepath for both loaded vehicle and unloaded vehicles, determine materials flow and movement for loaded vehicles (from/to chart) and determine movement for empty vehicles (from/to chart). From this information the number of vehicles required for the system is determined. The movement of empty vehicles is determined from a procedure called factoring.

Run Time (t$_R$)

The run time is the time, in minutes, the AGV requires to travel a specific "travel distance"—e.g., the time required for the vehicle to travel between inspection and final assembly. This is the actual time the vehicle is running; it does not include any deadhead time, idle time, blocking time, or P&D

time. The formula is: $t_R = d/v$, where $v =$ maximum veloc-
ity of AGV, feet/minute.

Blocking Time (t_b)

Blocking time is the time, in minutes, that a vehicle en
route must wait for other vehicles with the right-of-way to
clear an intersection, clear the P&D station, etc. This is
generally expressed as a function of the run time, usually
10% to 15% of the sum of the run time plus deadhead time.
The formula is: $t_b = .10(t_R + t_d)$

Idle Time (t_I)

The idle time is the time, in minutes, the vehicle is
parked and not utilized. The vehicle is available and waiting
for its next work assignment. This does not include the time
the vehicle is being maintained; the vehicle must be available
for work. This time is expressed as a function of the run
time, generally between 10% and 30%. The lower the
percent, the more demanding the system requirements;
these systems have the risk of extensive downtime if not
properly planned and executed. The formula is: $t_I = .20\, t_R$

P&D Time (t_p)

The P&D time is the time, in minutes, required for the
vehicle to pick up or deposit a load in a P&D station. This
includes vehicle creep time to position at the P&D station,
communication time between vehicles and controller, and
transfer time of the load. This is a constant time, generally
0.5 minutes to 1.5 minutes. Be careful to avoid unrealistic
P&D times. They can be the limiting factors, and the tendency is to use a fast P&D time.

Total Time (t_t)

The time required to complete one cycle of operation.
This is the summation of the run time + deadhead time +
blocking time + idle time + P&D time.
$(t_t = t_R + t_d + t_b + t_I + t_p)$.

Trips Per Shift Per AGV (T)

This is the number of trips one AGV can make in one shift of operation for a specific operation of the system. In referring to the example, each activity in the activity list has the number of trips per shift per AGV calculated. Sample calculation for "From-Receiving / To-Warehouse" activity list @ 100% capacity: T = Trips per shift per AGV = (number of minutes in one shift of operation) / (time for one AGV trip) = (60)(8)/13.25 = 36.22 trips per shift per AGV. These numbers were taken from the example below.

AGVs Per Shift

This is the number of AGVs required to achieve the throughput for one shift of operation. The summation of AGVs per shift indicates the number of AGVs required for the system. Sample calculation for "From-Receiving / To-Warehouse" activity list @ 100% capacity: AGVs per shift = (throughput) / (trips per shift per AGV) = (130)/(36.22) = 3.59 AGVs per shift. These numbers were taken from the example below.

Total Time AGV-Hours

This is the AGV-hours needed to handle the system requirements. When this quantity is known for all activities, the number of AGVs or the time per shift can be changed to determine the optimum results. In the example this quantity is not shown. The purpose of the calculation is to show which activity has the highest time requirement for the vehicle. In addition, the total AGV-hours for all activities is 213.7. Since there are 8 hours per shift of operation, a total of (213.7/8 = 26.71) 27 vehicles is required. AGV-hours = (throughput)(t_t)/60. Here is a sample calculation for "From-Receiving / To-Warehouse" @ 100% capacity: AGV-hours = (130)(13.25)/60 = 28.71 AGV-hours to do the task. These numbers were taken from the example below.

The first six activities for the "Activity list-100% capacity" are calculated and shown below:

Activity		Total Time AGV-Hours
From-Receiving	To-Warehouse	28.7
From-Warehouse	To-Production	29.1
From-Final Assembly	To-Shipping	34.6
From- Warehouse	To-Final Assembly	30.7
From-Production	To-Inspection	9.0
From-Warehouse	To-Shipping	13.0

If the list were continued, the total time for all activities would be 213.7 AGV-hours.

Actual Throughput for a Finite Number of AGVs (TP_m)

State the number of AGVs available. The maximum throughput rates can then be determined using the ratio of stated AGVs available to the actual number of vehicles calculated. TP_m= (available AGVs)(throughput per P&D)/ (total AGV/shift) i.e. TP_m=(27)(130)/26.7 = 131 P&Ds. These numbers were taken from the example below.

The following example goes through the mechanics of sizing the system using the methods and formulas outlined in this chapter. This large material delivery system would require a simulation to size the system. This example provides a rough guideline for how many vehicles may be required, points out that much of the vehicles' time is spent doing things besides transporting products, and shows how vehicle speed influences system throughput.

Example

A large manufacturing plant has six major departments to be serviced using an AGV system: receiving, warehouse, production, inspection, final assembly, and shipping. The travel distances between departments are typically several hundred feet. The system is laid out and the physical parameters cannot be changed. The throughput rates have been determined and listed in the material flow matrix, and the distances between departments appear in the activity list and spreadsheet. The throughput requirements are the average rates; it is estimated that the system could consistently exceed these requirements by 8% to 12%. From this information, make the necessary assumptions and determine the number of AGVs to support the throughput requirements. It is assumed that no buffer storage is required.

ASSUMPTION

AGV SPEED FPM	200.00
DEADHEAD TIME	0.60
BLOCKING TIME	0.12
IDLE TIME	0.25
P&D TIME MIN.	0.50
HRS./SHIFT	8.00
# OF AGVs	27.00
SYSTEM CAPACITY	1.00

Abbreviations Used in the Example:

RECEIVING	REC.
WAREHOUSE	WH
PRODUCTION	PROD
INSPECTION	INSPEC
FINAL ASSEMBLY	FASBY
SHIPPING	SHIP

MATERIAL FLOW MATRIX

FROM: TO:	REC.	WH	PROD	INSPEC	FASBY	SHIP	TOTAL
RECEIVING	*	130	12	4	18	6	170
WAREHOUSE	0	*	127	0	96	59	282
PRODUCTION	0	58	*	88	11	0	157
INSPECTION	0	34	16	*	52	0	102
FINAL ASSBLY	0	56	0	9	*	118	183
SHIPPING	13	5	0	0	0	*	18
TOTAL	13	283	155	101	177	183	912

Figure 9.3 TIME DISTRIBUTION-100%

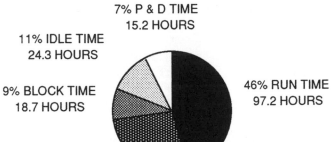

7% P & D TIME
15.2 HOURS

11% IDLE TIME
24.3 HOURS

9% BLOCK TIME
18.7 HOURS

46% RUN TIME
97.2 HOURS

27% DEAD HEAD TIME
58.3 HOURS

ACTIVITY LIST—AGV REQUIRED TO SUPPORT 100% CAPACITY

PICK UP	DE-POSIT	THRU PUT 1.00	TRV DIST. FEET	RUN TIME MIN.	DEAD HEAD MIN.	BLK TIME MIN.	IDLE TIME MIN.	TOTAL TIME AGV¹	TRIPS /SHIFT PER AGV	AGV PER SHIFT	THRU PUT/ 27 AGV
REC	WH	130	1200	6.00	3.60	1.15	1.50	13.25	36.22	3.6	131
WH	PROD	127	1250	6.25	3.75	1.20	1.56	13.76	34.88	3.6	128
FASB	SHIP	118	1625	8.13	4.88	1.56	2.03	17.59	27.29	4.3	119
WH	FASBY	96	1780	8.90	5.34	1.71	2.23	19.17	25.03	3.8	97
PROD	INSPEC	88	500	2.50	1.50	0.48	0.63	6.11	78.62	1.1	89
WH	SHIP	59	1200	6.00	3.60	1.15	1.50	13.25	36.22	1.6	60
PROD	WH	58	1250	6.25	3.75	1.20	1.56	13.76	34.88	1.7	59
FASBY	WH	56	1780	8.90	5.34	1.71	2.23	19.17	25.03	2.2	57
INSPEC	FASBY	52	790	3.95	2.37	0.76	0.99	9.07	52.95	1.0	53
INSPEC	WH	34	1200	6.00	3.60	1.15	1.50	13.25	36.22	0.9	34
REC	FASBY	18	2400	12.00	7.20	2.30	3.00	25.50	18.82	1.0	18
INSPEC	PROD	16	500	2.50	1.50	0.48	0.63	6.11	78.62	0.2	16
SHIP	REC	13	600	3.00	1.80	0.58	0.75	7.13	67.36	0.2	13
REC	PROD	12	2250	11.25	6.75	2.16	2.81	23.97	20.02	0.6	12
PROD	FASBY	11	625	3.13	1.88	0.60	0.78	7.38	65.03	0.2	11
FASBY	INSPEC	9	790	3.95	2.37	0.76	0.99	9.07	52.95	0.2	9
PROD	SHIP	6	1250	6.25	3.75	1.20	1.56	13.76	34.88	0.2	6
SHIP	WH	5	1200	6.00	3.60	1.15	1.50	13.25	36.22	0.1	5
REC	INSPEC	4	1700	8.50	5.10	1.63	2.13	18.36	26.15	0.2	4
TOTAL		912								26.7	922

1) Includes 1 minute for P&D time.

ACTIVITY LIST—AGV REQUIRED TO SUPPORT 112% CAPACITY

PICK UP	DE-POSIT	THRU PUT 1.12	TRV DIST. FEET	RUN TIME MIN.	DEAD HEAD MIN.	BLK TIME MIN.	IDLE TIME MIN.	TOTAL TIME AGV[1]	TRIPS /SHIFT PER AGV	THRU AGV PER SHIFT	PUT/ 30 AGV
REC	WH	146	1200	6.00	3.60	1.15	1.50	13.25	36.22	4.0	146
WH	PROD	142	1250	6.25	3.75	1.20	1.56	13.76	34.88	4.1	143
FASBY	SHIP	132	1625	8.13	4.88	1.56	2.03	17.59	27.29	4.8	133
WH	FASBY	108	1780	8.90	5.34	1.71	2.23	19.17	25.03	4.3	108
PRO	INSPEC	99	500	2.50	1.50	0.48	0.63	6.11	78.62	1.3	99
WH	SHIP	66	1200	6.00	3.60	1.15	1.50	13.25	36.22	1.8	66
PROD	WH	65	1250	6.25	3.75	1.20	1.56	13.76	34.88	1.9	65
FASBY	WH	63	1780	8.90	5.34	1.71	2.23	19.17	25.03	2.5	63
INSPEC	FASBY	58	790	3.95	2.37	0.76	0.99	9.07	52.95	1.1	58
INSPEC	WH	38	1200	6.00	3.60	1.15	1.50	13.25	36.22	1.1	38
REC	FASBY	20	2400	12.00	7.20	2.30	3.00	25.50	18.82	1.1	20
INSPEC	PROD	18	500	2.50	1.50	0.48	0.63	6.11	78.62	0.2	18
SHIP	REC	15	600	3.00	1.80	0.58	0.75	7.13	67.36	0.2	15
REC	PROD	13	2250	11.25	6.75	2.16	2.81	23.97	20.02	0.7	13
PROD	FASBY	12	625	3.13	1.88	0.60	0.78	7.38	65.03	0.2	12
FASBY	INSPEC	10	790	3.95	2.37	0.76	0.99	9.07	52.95	0.2	10
PROD	SHIP	7	1250	6.25	3.75	1.20	1.56	13.76	34.88	0.2	7
SHIP	WH	6	1200	6.00	3.60	1.15	1.50	13.25	36.22	0.2	6
REC	INSPEC	4	1700	8.50	5.10	1.63	2.13	18.36	26.15	0.2	4
TOTAL		1021								29.9	1024

1) Includes 1 minute for P&D time.

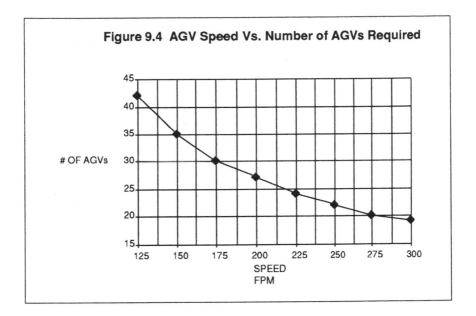

Figure 9.4 AGV Speed Vs. Number of AGVs Required

Discussion

Figure 9.3 shows the time distribution as a percent of the total available AGV hours for one shift of operation. It should be noted that the AGVs are actually used 45% of the total AGV time available. For a system of this size, with no buffer storage, it is a reasonable figure. If the system were smaller, the deadhead time could be reduced and the actual run time would be increased.

Depending on how often the system will run at the higher capacity (112%), the buyer may want to purchase extra vehicles. Extra vehicles are sometimes required for second shift operation. However, extra battery packs could be used to increase the utilization of the vehicles.

Figure 9.4 shows how speed affects the system requirements. It was constructed using the information and the assumptions in the above spreadsheets. The results indicate that a 25% increase in speed would yield 15% more throughput or 15% fewer AGVs required to support the system.

The main assumption was that the vehicle always travels at maximum speed, but this is not always the case. The

AGV must accelerate and decelerate, travel around curves and in reverse—all at much reduced speed. Also, if the pickup and delivery stations are close together, the vehicle would not achieve the maximum speed between stations.

Figure 9.4 shows how vendors could use higher speed equipment to reduce the number of vehicles in the system and reach a more competitive price. If a vendor uses speeds over 200 FPM, the buyer should make sure the vendor can demonstrate that he has successfully run at these speeds. Higher speed equipment must safely interface with people.

Recommendation

The above calculations indicate that the manufacturer should base the request for quote on purchasing 27 AGVs. Because of the size of the system, it would be strongly suggested that a simulation be run to optimize the overall system.

Estimating the System Price[7]

It is difficult to generalize about the cost of an AGV system; every system has its own unique features. In addition, each vendor uses different technology and techniques, which also influence the cost of an AGV system. Keep these limitations of a price estimating system in mind and use the guidelines with care. Both systems described below will produce a range of estimated prices.

The first price estimating system is based on only the number of vehicles in the system. The number of vehicles is multiplied by the number and the type of vehicle in the system. The procedure is as follows:

Method 1: Single Factor Price Estimating

Vehicle Type	Single Factor System Price Range
Driverless Tractors	$75,000 to $100,000
Pallet Vehicle	$40,000 to $60,000
Unit Load Under 1000 Pounds Capacity	$80,000 to $110,000
Unit Load Up to 4000 Pounds Capacity	$90,000 to $125,000
Fork Type Vehicle	$125,000 to $175,000
Heavy Capacity Vehicle Over 10,000 Pounds Capacity	$200,000 to $350,000

The second price estimating system is based on four parameters: the type of vehicle, the guidepath length, P&Ds, and design and installation services.

Method 2: Four Factor Price Estimating

FACTOR 1:

Vehicles with Battery Charger	Price Range
Driverless Tractors	$35,000 to $50,000
Pallet Vehicle	$25,000 to $40,000
Unit Load Under 1000 Pounds Capacity	$35,000 to $55,000
Unit Load Up to 4000 Pounds Capacity	$45,000 to $65,000
Fork Type Vehicle	$60,000 to $90,000
Heavy Capacity Vehicle Over 10,000 Pounds Capacity	$125,000 to $250,000

FACTOR 2:
Guidepath with Controls $20 to $50 per foot of
                                               guidepath

FACTOR 3:
P&D Stations with Load Presence Sensors

Frame on Floor $1000

Elevated Frame Stand $1,500 to $2,000

Single Position Powered
Roller Conveyor $5000 to $6,000

Extra Queue Positions $4,000 to $6,000

FACTOR 4:
**Design and Installation
Services**   15% to 25% of Factors 1,2,3

Example: Estimate the price of a system with the following
characteristics: 10 unit load vehicles with 2000 pound capacity, 11000 feet of guidepath, and 56 P&D stations (elevated
frame stand).

a) Using Method 1: Because of the high number of P&D
stations and extensive length of guidepath, the single price
factor should be toward the high point of the range. The
range for a unit load vehicle up to 4000 capacity is $90,000 to
$125,000; for this example use $120,000 per vehicle. Estimated system price is (10 vehicles)($120,000) = $1,200,000.

b) Using Method 2:

Factor 1:
10 unit load vehicles $50,000/vehicle $500,000

Factor 2:
11,000 feet of guidepath $30/feet $330,000

Factor 3:
56 elevated frame stand $1500/stand $84,000

Factor 4:
Design and installation   20%(Factor 1,2,3)
.2($914,000)   <u>$182,800</u>

Estimated System Price $1,096,800

It must be reemphasized that the results from these two pricing methods are *only estimates*; actual pricing must consider all elements of the AGV system. A comprehensive list of AGV system elements for pricing consideration is found in reference 8.

<u>REFERENCES</u>

1) A. Kuhn and F. Schmidt, "General EDP-Aided Planning and Realization of AGV-Systems," Fraunhofer-Institute for Transporttechnik and Warendistribution, West Germany. This paper was presented at the Third International Conference of Automated Guided Vehicles Systems, October 1985, Stockholm, Sweden.

2) R. Koether and F. Letters, "AGVS for Highly Productive Assembly Systems-A Sophisticated Simulation Tool to Optimize the System Design," Institute of Industrial Engineering (IAO), West Germany. This paper was presented at the Third International Conference of Automated Guided Vehicles Systems, October 1985, Stockholm, Sweden.

3) M. Annborn, "Automatic Trucks (AGV) for Flexible Material Handling in FMS Applications," AB Bygg-och Transportekonomi (BT), Sweden. This paper was presented at the Third International Conference of Automated Guided Vehicles Systems, October 1985, Stockholm, Sweden.

4) Tony Baer, "Simulating the Factory," *Mechanical Engineering*, December 1986, ASME, New York, New York.

5) Bruce J. Boldrin, Raymond Kulwiec (Editor), *Material Handling Handbook*, second edition, p. 308-309, 1985, John Wiley & Sons, New York, New York.

6) Omer Bakkalbasi, Leon F. McGinnis, "ABC's of Preliminary In-House Planning and Analysis of AGVS Applications," AGVS Proceeding 1989, Volume 1, p. 17, The Material Handling Institute, Charlotte, North Carolina.

7) Bruce J. Boldrin, "1989 AGVS Price Estimating Factors," AGV Technologies, Salt Lake City, Utah.

8) Guy Castleberry, *AGV System Specification, Procurement, and Implementation Guide*, 1990, Braun-Brumfield, Ann Arbor, Michigan. The book is distributed by AGV Decisions, 3616 E. Norport Drive, Port Washington, Wisconsin 53074.

INDEX

A

B

C